RECREATIONAL FOOTBALL

about the authors

Mildred (Mickey) Little is a professor of physical education at Texas A & M University and directs the Outdoor Education Institute. She taught physical education and coached at several secondary schools in Texas and at Mary Hardin-Baylor College in Belton, Texas, where she was head of the physical education department before joining the Texas A & M University faculty in 1971. Mickey received her doctorate from the University of Texas at Austin in 1969. As an undergraduate at the University of Texas she played and officiated touch football in the intramural program. She has published many articles on outdoor education and physical education, including contributions to four different NAGWS sport guides. Dr. Little is active in outdoor education and physical education professional associations in Texas and at the national level.

Linus J. Dowell received his doctorate from the University of Missouri in 1959 and served as Head of the Department of Health, Physical Education, and Recreation at Arkansas State University. Presently he is a professor of physical education at Texas A & M University and serves as coordinator of the graduate program. As an undergraduate at Northeast Missouri State University, Linus competed in athletics, lettered four years in football and track, and was the recipient of the Outstanding Athlete Award his senior year. He served four years in the United States Navy during the Korean war as an Operations Officer aboard the U.S.S. Navasota and after sea duty as Head Football Coach and Athletic Director at the United States Naval Preparatory School. Dr. Dowell has been active in professional associations at the state, district, and national levels and has published over 60 articles in professional journals and has authored or coauthored 7 books.

Jim Jeter is the Associate Director of Intramural and Recreational Sports at Texas A & M University and spent two years at Fort Hood, Texas, where he served as Athletic Specialist for the First Cavalry Division. Jim is state representative for NIRSA and has made many presentations at state and national conferences. He has played and officiated flag football and flickerball over the last 8 years. Jim has been responsible for training officials for Texas A & M's intramural flag football and flickerball program, which has over 500 teams each year.

RECREATIONAL FOOTBALL

Flag, Touch, and Flicker

Physical Education Activities Series

MILDRED J. LITTLE
Texas A & M University

LINUS J. DOWELL
Texas A & M University

JAMES M. JETER
Texas A & M University

Wm. C. Brown Company Publishers
Dubuque, Iowa

Consulting Editors

Physical Education
    Aileene Lockhart
    Texas Woman's University

Health
    Robert Kaplan
    The Ohio State University

Parks and Recreation
    David Gray
    California State University, Long Beach

Copyright © 1980 by Wm. C. Brown Company Publishers

Library of Congress Catalog Card Number: 79-55493

ISBN 0-697-07092-1

Printed in the United States of America

contents

preface

An increased interest in recreational football has become keenly evident in recent years. This enthusiasm can be attributed to the tremendous growth of regulation football as well as to the existence of the football "mystique" of our society.

Slightly different rules for touch, flag, and coed football are used in different parts of the country, but in general, most groups agree on certain fundamentals. REC football, as described in this book, incorporates the best of these rules and is designed to allow for the most enjoyable, least dangerous, and most compatible game possible. The advantages for having uniformity in the rules so that men and women play by identical rules and so that the game can be played as either flag or touch are numerous. REC football offers a challenging game for coed groups also.

Flag and touch football are not games of strength; they are games of skill and finesse. The more proficient a player becomes in the fundamental skills, the more valuable he/she becomes to the team. Over 50 percent of the game is fundamental skill; the rest includes execution, teamwork, and strategy. The fundamental skills may be learned and developed effectively and pleasurably through a variety of practice activities, such as the drills and relays presented in chapter 5 and the football related games presented in chapter 7.

Since flickerball has become such a popular football related team sport and is played in numerous physical education activity classes and intramural programs, an entire chapter has been devoted to the rules and officiating. Flickerball and REC football are both exciting to play, since they are rich in strategy and teams are challenged to make up all sorts of plays in an attempt to outwit their opponents.

This text is designed for physical education classes, intramural and other recreational programs, for men and women, boys and girls, and coed groups alike. The intrinsic value of competition, skills, strategy, ability to run and think, excitement in moving, and the thrill of competition all add to the reason why REC football is the sport for today's youth.

Appreciation is expressed to the American Alliance for Health, Physical Education, and Recreation for permission to use 3 football skill tests from the *Football Skills Test Manual* (1966). Special thanks are extended to Ms. Carolyn Hewatt and to the Division of Recreational Sports at The University of Texas for the use of the photographs appearing on pages 14 and 18. The Office of Intramurals and Recreational Sports at Texas A & M University provided all the other photographs. Gratitude is also expressed to Mrs. Celia Jeter for the diagrams.

introduction to rec football

1

Recreational football is an outgrowth of regulation football, which began in the United States over one hundred years ago. Through the years football has changed from a game similar to soccer to a game that brought about the flying wedge, the forward pass, the seven-man line, quarters instead of halves, and other changes that opened the game up, made it safer, increased spectator interest, and increased the use of strategy and organization. The American game today is definitely an American development and no longer resembles the English game of rugby, from which American football developed.

Today's young men and women, who enjoy the skills of the game of football but who do not have the opportunity or the desire to play on organized football teams, have modified the game of regulation football: first into touch football; then into flag football; and now into coed football. Because of the absence of protective equipment, obviously some rules of regulation football had to change for the sake of safety.

Men and women have played intramural touch football in college and university intramural programs since the 1940s. "Powder Puff" games were extremely popular, and increased requests for standardized rules of a football-type game for women resulted in a study in 1967 by the Division of Girls and Women's Sports of the American Association for Health, Physical Education, and Recreation. As a result of investigating various rules on campuses where a football-type game was played, DGWS selected flag football. The first flag football rules were used experimentally in 1969 and the first national rules for women were published by DGWS in 1970. This organization, now known as the National Association for Girls and Women in Sport, publishes the rules in June of even numbered years in the *Soccer-Speedball-Flag Football Guide*.

Other sources for rules include the Athletic Institute's book entitled *The Official National Touch and Flag Football Rules*; a brief section in the National Federation of State High School Associations' *Football Handbook*; and Flag-A-Tag's rule book, *Flag Football*.

The game of recreational football (hereafter called REC football) incorporates the best of the rules of touch and flag football for men and women and offers a challenging game for coed groups. REC football is played by two teams of seven players each. However, the game may be adapted for nine or eleven players each. The object is to score touchdowns by running or passing the ball over the opponent's goal line.

The playing field consists of a field of 100 yards from end line to end line and 50 yards in width. The end zones are 10 yards in depth, leaving a playing field 80 yards in length. The playing field is divided into quarters of 20 yards each. (Fig. 3.1).

Equipment needed is minimal. A football of regulation or intermediate size may be used. If the flag football version is played, two flags on a belt or two flags tucked in a belt constitute the essential equipment. Usually the flags are from 13-to-16-inches long and contrasting in color for each team. A downs marker indicating the number of downs used, a marker to indicate where a series of downs originated, and a timing device, usually a stop watch or a game clock are needed. It is recommended that the game be played on a grass field or artificial turf and that playing apparel include long pants. Usually colored shirts, scrimmage vests, or pinnies are worn to differentiate teams. Players may wear soccer-type shoes with soft soles and soft rubber cleats or tennis shoes. Spiked shoes or barefooted players should not be allowed. Glass guards are recommended when glasses are worn. Pads and helmets are prohibited.

The game of REC football consists of two 25-minute halves with 5 minutes between halves. Each team is allowed two time-outs of one minute duration each half. Up to 25 seconds is allowed to snap the ball during any scrimmage play. The clock runs continuously during the game.

Methods of scoring include the touchdown, the conversion, and the safety. Moving the ball on possession from the field of play into the end zone, i.e., the touchdown, counts 6 points. A successful conversion after a touchdown counts 2 points if the ball penetrates the goal line and 1 point if it penetrates the 5-yard line. Stopping your opponent behind their goal line, i.e., the safety, counts 2 points.

The game begins with the ball on the 20-yard line of the team having gained possession through the coin toss. A team has four downs to advance the ball into the next zone, at which time a new series of downs is awarded. All kicks are announced kicks. The ball is dead whenever it touches the ground. Hence, there is no "free" ball on a kicked ball touching the ground or a fumbled ball touching the ground. The ball is dead and play is stopped anytime a flag is pulled or a player is touched, depending on the method designated to down the ball carrier.

Skills of running, passing, receiving, centering, and blocking by body position alone are used by the offensive team. Rushing, pass defense, flag pulling or touching, and intercepting passes are skills used by the defensive team. Body contact is not permitted when blocking, pulling the flag, or touching. Other skills needed on special occasions include punting, placekicking, receiving a kicked ball, lateral passing, handing off, ball carrying, and broken field running.

Linemen on offense may be designated as right end, center, and left end or as right end, right guard, center, left guard, and left end on a 7-man team. The quarterback and the halfback may comprise the backfield of a 7-man team

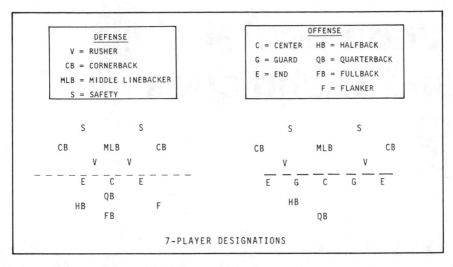

Figure 1.1

or it may consist of the quarterback, halfback, fullback, and flanker. Players on defense are designated as defensive linemen (rushers), cornerbacks, safeties, and middle linebacker (Fig. 1.1). These positions may change somewhat depending on the down, score, time left in the game, strategy, etc.

Many of the values of REC football are unique. Through increased knowledge of terms, strategy, and rules, interest as a spectator of regulation football will increase. REC football affords wholesome competition that contributes to respect for teammates. The development of running, passing, and kicking skills, as well as agility, balance, and body control contribute to the player's motor fitness and physiological fitness.

fundamental skills and techniques

2

Many of the skills and techniques of regulation football are used in REC football. The areas of difference are greatest in the method of downing the ball carrier and blocking. As in any sport, the more proficient a player becomes in the fundamental skills the more valuable he/she becomes to the team. Over 50 percent of the game is fundamental skill; the rest includes excution, teamwork, and strategy. If each player masters the fundamental skills, his team is on its way to victory. Practice in the following fundamentals is essential to a good REC football team.

STANCE

The basic football stance provides the foundation for movement. It is important that the stance taken be one from which you can move quickly and still be aware of movement in the field of play.

Offensive Stance

Interior linemen must be in a stance that will allow them to move laterally or backwards as quickly as possible. Since contact is not allowed, they must move to make the defensive player take the longest path to the ball carrier.

Interior Linemen

1. Feet are spread shoulder width apart, weight evenly distributed.
2. Feet should be flat on the ground with heel-to-toe stagger, inside foot forward.
3. Inside foot must be on the line of scrimmage.
4. Back is straight with head up, eyes looking straight ahead.
5. Knees are slightly flexed.
6. In set position, hands are placed on knees.

Ends

1. Feet are spread less than shoulder width, approximately 12 inches.
2. Feet staggered a little more than heel-toe relationship.
3. Weight is evenly distributed between both feet and placed on the balls of the feet.
4. Inside foot should be on the line of scrimmage.
5. Back is straight with head up, eyes looking straight ahead.
6. Knees are slightly flexed.
7. In set position, arms are hung loosely in front, but still.

Center

1. Feet are placed extremely wide apart and on the same line, hips high, weight equally distributed on both feet.
2. Bend knees slightly.
3. Head is up, eyes looking straight ahead.
4. In T formation left arm rests on left leg above knee, right hand is around nose of football.
5. In centering to deep back, both hands are on ball; right hand over nose of ball, left hand over center top of ball, used as guide.

Backs

1. Feet are spread less than shoulder width, approximately 12 inches.
2. Feet are staggered a little more than heel-toe relationship with outside foot forward.
3. Weight is evenly distributed between both feet and on balls of feet.
4. Back is straight, legs only slightly flexed, head up with entire defensive team in field of vision.
5. Hands are on knees in T formation. Arms are cradled across thighs, palms facing forward if deep back in single- or double-wing formation.

Offensive Stance Tips

1. Be comfortable in stance.
2. Be relaxed but mentally alert.
3. Adjust feet before assuming defensive position.

The placement of the feet in the offensive stance differs according to the player's position. How should your feet be placed if you are an Interior Lineman? An End? The Center? A Back?

---

4. Feet and lower legs should be parallel.
5. Head is up, eyes looking directly ahead.
6. Weight is evenly distributed between feet.

7. Be in a position to move quickly in any direction.
8. Do not tip off play by leaning, pointing with eyes, head, body, or face expression.

Defensive Stance

The defensive line stance is similar to the offensive line stance, except that the center of gravity is well forward so that forward movement may be initiated as soon as the ball is snapped.

Defensive Linemen

1. Feet are spread about shoulder width.
2. Outside foot is slightly forward.
3. Weight is evenly distributed with weight forward on balls of feet.
4. Back is straight with head up, eyes looking at ball and backfield.
5. Knees are slightly flexed.
6. Hands and arms are relaxed to aid in initial movement.

Defensive Backs

1. Feet are spread less than shoulder width.
2. Outside foot slightly forward.
3. Weight is evenly distributed between feet.
4. Body is erect, back straight, head up, eyes on offensive backs with ends in field of vision.
5. Hands and arms are relaxed.
6. Weight is over feet in position to move in any direction.

Defensive Stance Tips

1. Be relaxed but mentally alert.
2. Lineman should have center of gravity well forward.
3. Backs should display split vision to see entire field of play.
4. Lineman should display split vision to see snap of ball and backfield.

PASSING

REC football emphasizes the use of the forward pass (Fig. 2.1). Completed passes make yardage quickly and with relative ease. Passes also loosen up the defense and make running more effective. Passes should be mixed with the running game in order to keep the defense guessing. The defense may be able to stop a running attack if they know a team will run, or may be able to cover passes if they know a team will pass. Therefore, it is important to conceal the type of play called and not "give it away."

Figure 2.1

Forward Pass

1. Grip ball slightly behind the middle of the ball with fingers on and across the lace.
2. Carry ball high with both hands on ball.
3. Focus on target and rotate body away from target.
4. Plant same foot as throwing arm.
5. Bring ball back beyond ear, upper arm parallel to ground.
6. Step directly toward target with foot opposite throwing arm.
7. Whip ball forward past ear with elbow leading.
8. Snap wrist downward on releasing ball to impart spin.
9. Follow through with arm toward target, palm rotated outward.
10. End follow-through with weight on forward foot.

Lateral Pass—Two-Hand Chest

1. Grasp ball in center with both hands.
2. Eyes on receiver.
3. Bring ball to chest and step toward receiver.
4. Thrust ball outward toward receiver, extending arms toward target as in basketball chest pass.
5. Palms of hands follow through turned outward, weight on forward foot.
6. Pass ball without spiral toward chest of receiver.

Lateral Pass—Two-Arm Underhand

1. Grasp ball with both hands toward tip of ball.
2. With eyes on receiver, step toward receiver on opposite leg from ball.
3. Bring ball down and back and step forward, shovel pass ball underhanded to receiver.
4. Pass dead ball end first to receiver about waist height.
5. Follow through extending arms toward receiver and transferring weight to forward foot.

Lateral Pass—One-Hand Underhanded

1. Ball is in dominant hand held slightly behind center.
2. Stay low with knees flexed and hop-step toward receiver.
3. Bring ball behind body for good arc.
4. Swing arm and ball forward pendulumlike toward receiver.
5. Lift up with fingers as ball is released to impart spin to ball.
6. Aim for waist of receiver; follow through by transferring weight to forward leg and pointing arm toward receiver.

Passing Tips

1. Look for the defensive man as well as the receiver.
2. Learn the speed of receivers.
3. Fake realistically to help receivers get free.
4. Have firm grip on ball for passing as soon as possible.
5. Throw ball to side of receiver away from defender.
6. Learn the defensive men who are weak on covering pass receivers.
7. Stay in the blocker's pocket while passing.
8. Know where each receiver is during a pass route.
9. If receivers are covered, attempt a run and then throw.
10. Before throwing, set up by planting a foot.

The position of the feet in the offensive or defensive stance makes a difference in speed of take-off. Which player is in the least advantageous position for moving quickly? Why?

RECEIVING PASSES

Above the Waist

1. Get in position in front of ball.
2. Reach out for ball, fingers spread and relaxed, thumbs in, and palms forward facing oncoming ball (fig. 2.2).
3. Look ball into hands.
4. Fingers, hands, and arms give with the ball on contact.
5. Tuck ball away in carrying position.
6. Continue run downfield.

Figure 2.2

Below the Waist

1. Get in position in front of ball.
2. Reach out in front for ball, fingers spread and pointed down, palms toward oncoming ball, little fingers together; relax.
3. Look ball into hands.
4. Fingers, hands, and arms give with ball on contact.
5. Tuck ball away.
6. Continue run downfield.

Over the Shoulder

1. Judge flight of the ball.
2. Outstretch arms, fingers spread, little fingers together forming a basket for the ball, palms up.
3. Look ball into hands.
4. Give with the ball on contact.
5. Tuck ball away.
6. Continue run.

Receiving Tips

1. Keep eyes on the ball.
2. Be ready to change directions if necessary.
3. Keep your body between the ball and the defender.
4. Maintain control of the body position at all times.
5. Catch ball at longest point from body.
6. Relax to cushion the ball on contact.
7. Wrap fingers around ball and tuck away before continuing run downfield.

Accuracy and distance in passing or kicking result from much practice. Ask a partner to receive for you. Make three forward passes and then three punts and record the best distance for each. Keep a record for several weeks to note improvement as skill increases.

---

8. Run in straight-line patterns rather than circles.
9. Fake realistically using head and shoulders; change direction and speed to get open.
10. If unable to catch pass, be in a position to make sure defender is also unable to catch pass.

CENTERING

The play of the center is most important for the proper execution of play. The center initiates play, and accurate delivery between the center and quarterback or between the center and deep back dictates the effectiveness of the play. Proper execution between the center and receiver comes through proper technique and extensive practice.

Deep Snap

1. Assume stance, feet wide apart, head up, hips high, weight equally distributed.
2. Both hands are on ball, dominant hand over ball toward nose of football, other hand is on top of ball at center to be used as a guide.
3. Fingers of dominant hand are over lace of ball.
4. Pass ball between legs as upside-down forward pass.
5. On an end run lead the runner slightly so he/she can catch the ball in stride.
6. Keep the ball about waist high and get ball to runner quickly but not too hard.
7. When centering to fullback or punter, center directly so receiver will receive the ball about knee high.

Direct Snap

1. Assume stance, feet wide apart, head up, hips high, weight equally distributed.
2. Dominant hand is around forward end of football, laces up, other arm rests on left leg above the knee.
3. On count, snap ball between legs rotating ball 90 degrees to quarterback's hands.
4. Center should give the quarterback the ball with laces up and longitudinal axis of the football parallel to the line of scrimmage.

Centering Tips

1. Make passes accurately.
2. Practice extensively with receivers.
3. Do not point the ball.

Regardless of type, there are principles that apply to all passes. Can you name several?

---

4. Do not pick the ball up and move it.
5. Swing arms freely through legs.
6. Follow the ball to deep back, wrists loose.
7. Pass well before blocking.

RECEIVING SNAP

Quarterback (fig. 2.3)

1. Take square stance, close to center, feet parallel at about shoulder width and toes parallel to line of scrimmage.
2. Knees are bent, back is straight, head is up looking at defense.
3. Dominant hand is up under center, palm facing down, fingers spread and relaxed.
4. Other hand is palm facing forward with heel of hand touching heel of dominant hand, fingers spread and relaxed.
5. Ball is centered with laces up into dominant hand so fingers fall across laces in position for passing.
6. Hands give with ball to guide it into body.

Deep Back

1. Take deep back stance, arms on inside of thighs, palms facing forward, outside foot forward.
2. Keep eyes on the ball.
3. On snap take short drive step with inside foot, driving off outside foot.
4. Extend outside arms, palm of hand facing oncoming ball, fingers spread.

Figure 2.3

5. Inside arm is parallel with outside arm extended forward, palm up, forming basket with backboard.
6. As ball makes contact, give with ball.
7. Pull ball into body.
8. For running plays tuck ball away, outside hand over nose of ball, tip of ball in armpit.

Receiving Snap Tips

1. Keep relaxed.
2. Keep hands around ball.
3. Tuck ball away on running plays.
4. Line up in the same position each time.
5. Look downfield.
6. Don't point or give play away.
7. On the direct snap, don't move out before snap is completed.
8. Don't fumble.

HAND-OFF

All backs must learn to take the ball properly from the quarterback. The majority of fumbles occur during the exchange of the football between quarterback and halfbacks. It is very important to the running game to make a fluid hand-off so that split-second timing may be effected. Too often games are lost because teams did not perfect their ball exchanges.

Quarterback Hand-Off

1. Receive ball from center as receiving snap.
2. Bring ball to body, take step with foot nearest direction of hand-off.
3. Drive off back foot.
4. Grasp hand around center of ball with hand closest to line of scirmmage.
5. Extend ball and softly place in stomach of receiver.
6. Let back receiving ball take it out of your hand.

Receiving Hand-Off

1. Inside forearm is up, parallel to ground across chest, palm open and facing down.
2. Outside forearm across abdomen parallel to ground, palm open and facing up toward inside elbow.
3. Lean forward as quarterback places ball in stomach, enclose around ball.
4. Grasp end of ball with outside hand and place other end in armpit.
5. Place inside hand on top of ball to protect it.
6. Look straight ahead.

Hand-Off Tips

1. Hand-offs and fake hand-offs should look the same to the defense.
2. Quarterback and receiver of hand-off should reach the point of exchange at the same time. Timing is of the essence.
3. After the hand-off is made, fakes must be carried out.

KICKING

Punting and kicking play an important part in any ball game. In REC Football a team will kick an average of six to ten times during a game. This gives 12 to 20 times that a kick plays an important part in the game. Field position is either won or lost through the kicking game. Kicking is a highly specialized skill and adherence to the fundamental techniques is necessary.

Punting

1. Since there is no rush on punts, stand upright with arms outstretched toward oncoming ball a minimum distance from the line of scrimmage.
2. Right foot is slightly in front of left in normal standing position.
3. Take a short step with right foot as ball approaches.
4. Catch ball in outstretched hands; give with ball.
5. Rotate ball until laces are up and slightly to the outside.
6. Hold ball with both hands, right hand on outside of rear of ball, left hand on inside forward.
7. Hop on left foot and cock right foot to gluteal muscles.
8. Ball is pointed down toward kicking foot, drop ball on foot.
9. Ball is contacted diagonally across instep of kicking foot.
10. Follow through with kicking foot, right leg locked on contact.
11. Right foot ends up over left shoulder (fig. 2.4).
12. Because of explosive power in the kicking leg, as leg locks upward the whole body is lifted off the ground, arms move outward to maintain balance.

Placekick

1. Adjust distance so that on run through, left leg will land beside ball.
2. The ball is held by the safety man at a 60 degree angle, or placed in a kick-off tee.
3. The kicking leg is cocked back at the knee at about a 45 degree angle with the right ankle locked forming a right angle with the lower leg.
4. The toe of the kicking foot meets the ball below its middle point with the leg swinging through in a straight line.
5. The kick should be high and deep since the ball is declared dead when it hits the ground.

Figure 2.4

Kicking Tips

1. Develop good kicking form.
2. Be relaxed.
3. Step in the direction of the kick.
4. Kick low into the wind and high with the wind.
5. Check on protection and coverage.
6. Keep eyes on the ball until it is kicked.
7. Snap the lower leg and contact the ball with toe extended when punting and at right angles when placekicking.
8. Punt from close to the line of scrimmage to get greater distance and take advantage of the rules.
9. Get downfield fast after kicking.
10. Punt out-of-bounds when advantageous.

RECEIVING KICKS

Punts and Placekicks

1. Play back beyond range of punter and move up with the punt.
2. Move quickly to spot where ball will hit the ground.
3. Keep eyes on ball at all times.
4. Extend arms, forearms outstretched and parallel, palms upward, fingers spread and relaxed, form basket.
5. Watch ball into arms.
6. Give with ball and pull ball to body.
7. Place dominant hand over nose of ball and place other end of ball in armpit.

8. Cover ball with other hand for protection.
9. Move up field as broken field runner.

OFFENSE PLAY

REC Football does not allow for contact blocking. But since the offense must have time enough to execute plays, it is advantageous for them to make it as difficult as possible for the defense to upset the quarterback before he/she has time to get rid of the ball. Obviously a team must score to win ball games, making it imperative to perfect the selection and execution of plays.

Line Play

1. Take lineman's stance, feet parallel, shoulder width apart.
2. Weight is evenly distributed on both feet, back straight, head up, hands on knees.
3. On snap of ball move to position in front of defensive lineman, hands behind back (fig. 2.5).
4. Since contact is not allowed, don't go after defensive man but let defensive man come to you; move to cut-off point between him/her and quarterback.
5. Anticipate defensive man's movement and plan to screen him/her from ball carrier.

Ball Carrying

1. Hold ball firmly with palm of hand around nose of ball.
2. Carry ball in arm away from nearest opponent.
3. Hold tightly against body with end of ball in armpit.

Figure 2.5

You are about to punt. How will you aim if the wind is with you? If you are kicking into the wind? Where should you stand to punt in relation to the line of scrimmage?

4. Protect ball with other hand when in heavy traffic.
5. In open field be ready to side-step right or left.
6. Be ready to pivot in either direction.
7. Follow your interference.

Offense Tips

1. Be alert at all times, ready to outguess the defensive man.
2. When you catch a defensive man off balance, break.
3. Always protect the ball.
4. Mix plays to keep the defense guessing.
5. Vary distance between players in the line to confuse the intent of the offense.

DEFENSE PLAY

Defense is an important aspect of the game. If you can keep your opponents from scoring you will be hard to beat. The defense needs to work as a team. If a player moves out of an area, other members of the team must cover the area vacated. Defense coverage and application of pressure on the quarterback is an important part of REC Football. This aspect of the game should not be overlooked.

Line Play

1. Take defensive stance, outside foot forward, weight on balls of feet, lean forward, arms relaxed.
2. Be ready to charge as soon as ball moves.
3. Keep quarterback to your inside.
4. Learn to fake and spin out to avoid making contact with blocker and get behind him/her.
5. Move to put pressure on quarterback so he/she will have to rush the play (fig. 2.6).
6. On rushing passer, keep arms high to make quarterback pass over.

Linebacker Play

1. Linebacker's first responsibility is to cover his/her area for a pass.
2. If shooting the gap to get to a passer, play should be set up so your pass area is covered by teammates.
3. Keep quarterback and potential pass receivers in your area in field of vision.
4. Back up if pass is indicated and then come up or move laterally to cover man in your area.

Figure 2.6

5. Don't move on head fakes; make sure hips move in that direction before going.

Covering or Guarding

1. Take waiting position, outside foot forward, weight evenly distributed, standing erect, arms hanging, relaxed.
2. Watch potential receiver, but keep quarterback in field of vision.
3. Judge offensive receiver's speed and play accordingly.
4. Don't let receiver in your area get behind you before the ball is thrown.
5. Don't move on head fakes; make sure hips move in that direction before going.
6. As soon as ball is thrown, move to intercept or tip ball.
7. Reach out to tip ball as soon as possible and at farthest point from body (fig. 2.7).

Defense Tips

1. Start fast on all plays.
2. Fake blockers and move to make ball carrier declare his/her direction.
3. Observe the offensive formation and position of players.
4. Watch for clues and tip-offs to the play.
5. Never leave your feet.
6. Vary your rushing routes.
7. Go in fast to prevent the play from developing.

Figure 2.7

8. Anticipate a play coming back your way.
9. Vary your style of defensive play, move out and set, move out and come back, move and dart through the split.
10. Vary your style of defensive play according to the position of the ball on the field, down, time remaining, etc.
11. Fake a charge at potential receiver and move back to cover before ball is snapped.

DOWNING THE BALL CARRIER

Downing the ball carrier may take one of two forms: the one-hand touch anywhere or the pulling of a flag are the most common. Since downing the ball carrier is where some contact takes place and injuries often occur, a quick whistle should result if the downing is not performed according to the rules. Skill is important for proper execution.

Touching

1. Move to ball carrier with maximum speed and body control.
2. When in proximity of ball carrier, assume a wide base, lower center of gravity, and spread arms.
3. Keep head up and eye contact on waist of ball carrier.
4. Be ready for any fake movement and don't get off balance by following a fake movement.
5. Get close enough to ball carrier so you don't have to leave your feet.
6. Tag ball carrier anywhere rules permit.

Figure 2.8

Pulling Flag

1. Run fast to ball carrier keeping body under control.
2. Get close enough to ball carrier so you can grab flag without leaving feet.
3. When fairly close to ball carrier, spread feet, flex knees, keep back straight, head up, arms outstretched, and eyes on midsection of ball carrier (fig. 2.8).
4. Anticipate any fake moves and keep eyes on flags.
5. Let offensive ball carrier make initial move and break before attempting to pull flag.
6. Reach out quickly, grasp flag, and give it a yank.
7. Hold the flag high overhead at the spot where it was pulled.

Tips

1. Keep body control with speed at all times.
2. Keep head up, eyes on target, and back straight.
3. Widen base close to ball carrier to avoid being faked off balance.
4. Timing of touch or pulling of flag is essential.
5. Never leave your feet when downing the ball carrier.

SUMMARY

REC Football is based on the proper execution of the skills and techniques described in this chapter. The higher the level of skill developed in these fundamentals the greater will be the satisfaction of participation.

Skill in the various fundamentals are developed through practice. Teams should become acquainted with drills designed to improve skill in each of the fundamentals.

If your team will practice the drills described in chapter 5 and work to improve the level of skill in each of the fundamentals presented in this chapter, you will find increased enjoyment in REC Football competition.

rec football rules and officiating

3

REC Football is closely associated with regulation football, but since players wear no protective padding of any kind, it is necessary to modify certain rules for player safety. REC Football rules were developed after considerable study of existing flag and touch football rules used for both men and women and for coed teams in colleges, high schools, and various recreation programs. The rules were designed to allow for the most enjoyable, least dangerous, and most compatible game possible. The advantages for having uniformity in the rules so that men and women play by identical rules and so that the game can be played as either flag or touch are numerous and quite understandable.

It is recommended that REC Football teams be comprised of 7 players rather than 9 or 11 players for the following reasons:

1. There is less chance of accidental collision.
2. There is less confusion since the playing area is small.
3. The number of receivers and defenders closely resembles that of regulation football.
4. The game is more exciting and higher scoring results.
5. The smaller number of players allows for more teams.

Other rules that eliminate much of the physical contact of other games include that of no blocking and the fact that all balls that touch the ground are dead.

Every effort has been made to simplify and condense the rules, but repetition has been necessary in some instances to facilitate a thorough understanding. As an aid to those who officiate REC Football, the official's hand signals are incorporated with the rules. REC Football has its hazards, but if properly coached, officiated, and directed the injury rate is negligible.

OFFICIAL REC FOOTBALL RULES

The object of the game is to score touchdowns by running or passing the ball over the opponent's goal line.

Rule 1. The Game, Field, Players, and Equipment

Section 1 REC Football is a game played by two teams of seven players each. A team must have seven players to begin a contest but may complete a contest with fewer than seven.

Section 2 The teams shall be awarded points for scoring according to the rules. Unless the game is forfeited, the team having the larger score at the end of the game shall be the winning team.

Section 3 Each team manager or coach shall designate to the referee a team captain who will speak for the team in dealing with officials. A field captain's first choice of any option shall be irrevocable.

Section 4 The field shall be a rectangular area with lines and zones as shown in Figure 3.1. In case of space limitations, the length and width of the field can be modified.

Section 5 Soft, flexible pylons or flags with flexible staffs should be placed at the inside corners of the four intersections of the goal lines and sidelines.

Section 6 The official football shall be either leather or rubber covered and shall be of regulation size or intermediate size, depending on the age and skill level of the players. A striped ball is recommended for night play.

Section 7 Players of opposing teams must wear shirts, scrimmage vests, or pinnies of contrasting colors. The referee shall designate which team shall make a change, if necessary.

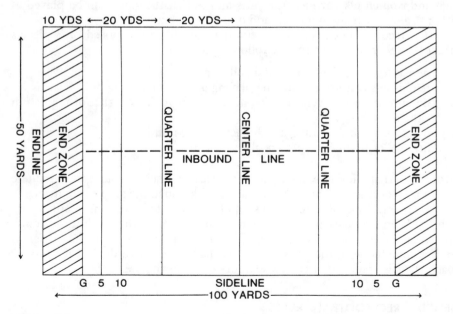

Figure 3.1

Section 8   When playing the flag version of REC Football, each player on the field will wear a belt at his/her waistline with two flags attached but not tied thereto. Each flag should extend or hang from the waist a minimum of 13 inches on each side of the body. Flags should be 3 inches wide and 13-to-16-inches long.

Section 9   No player wearing illegal equipment shall be permitted to play. The umpire will decide the legality of all equipment. Illegal equipment shall include:

A. Any equipment that in the opinion of the umpire could confuse or endanger other players.
B. Helmets; padded uniforms; or leather or other hard or unyielding substance on the hands, wrist, forearms or elbows, no matter how well covered or padded.
C. Any metal shoe cleats, as distinguished from regulation molded soccer-type shoes.
D. Wrapping, tying, or in any way securing the flags to the uniform or belt, other than prescribed by rule. Intentionally removing a flag during play is illegal.

PENALTY: 15 yards and possible disqualification (Rule 1, Section 9D)
OFFICIAL HAND SIGNAL: UNSPORTSMANLIKE CONDUCT

Rule 2.   Definitions

See glossary.

Rule 3.   Scoring

Section 1   The following system shall be used in scoring a game.

A. Touchdown .... 6 points
B. Safety .... 2 points
C. Successful conversion: The ball is placed on the 10-yard line for a conversion attempt and may be moved by either passing or running. Points are scored according to the distance covered before the ball is declared dead.
    1. 10 yards .... 2 points
    2. 5 yards .... 1 point
D. Forfeited game 1-0
E. Penetration (tie game) .... 1 point

OFFICIAL HAND SIGNAL:
          TOUCHDOWN OR CONVERSION   SAFETY

Section 2   When the game ends in a tie score, the team with the greatest number of 20-yard penetrations shall be the winner.

Section 3   If both teams have the same number of 20-yard penetrations the following method shall be used to determine a winner.

A. A coin toss shall be made between the two field captains to determine which team shall make the first play and the direction the play shall begin.
B. Starting at midfield, a series of 8 alternating downs are played, the team ending in the opponent's territory being credited with one point.
C. In case of a touchdown the try for point is attempted and the ball is returned to midfield and given to the team whose turn it is at the time.
D. If the ball ends up at midfield, a one-minute intermission is taken and the overtime procedure is repeated, except that a series of only four alternating plays are made.

Rule 4.   Periods, Time Factors, and Substitutions

Section 1   The game shall consist of two 25-minute halves with 5 minutes between halves. The clock shall run continuously.

Section 2   Each half shall start with the ball on the 20-yard line of the team having gained possession through the coin toss. Three minutes before the start of the game, the referee shall toss a coin, after first designating which captain shall call the toss.

A. The captain winning the toss shall have the choice of one of the following options: offense, defense, or to defend a goal. The losing captain shall have the choice of the remaining options.
B. Before the start of the second half, the choosing of the options will be reversed.

   *Section 3*   Each team is allowed two time-outs of one minute duration per half. Approximately five minutes before the end of each half both team captains will be informed that five minutes remain and that no time-outs will be allowed.

Section 4   Any number of legal substitutes for either team may enter the game between periods, after a score or conversion, or during the interval between downs.

Section 5   Delay of game violations:

A. Not having all players on the field and ready to play; delaying the start of each half.
B. Consuming more than 25 seconds in putting the ball in play after it is ready for play.
C. Failing to remove an injured player for whom a free time-out is awarded.
D. Deliberately advancing the ball after it has been blown dead.
E. Causing undue delay of regular play in the judgment of the official.

PENALTY: 5 yards (Rule 4, Section 5)
OFFICIAL HAND SIGNAL: DELAY OF GAME

Rule 5.   Ball In Play, Dead Ball, and Out of Bounds

Section 1   A dead ball, after having been declared ready for play, becomes a live ball when it is snapped or free kicked legally or illegally.

Section 2   A live ball becomes dead when:

A. It goes out of bounds or crosses a goal line or end line.
B. Any part of a ball carrier other than his/her feet touches the ground.
C. A legal ball carrier is touched or has one of his/her flags pulled.
D. The ball hits the ground, be it passed, kicked, fumbled, or muffed. The ball is dead at the spot of contact except that a ball fumbled forward is considered dead at the spot where fumbled.
E. Any portion of a ball carrier touches the sideline, end line, territory, or fixture outside of these lines.
F. A pass is completed to a receiver who comes down with one foot in fair territory and one foot in foul territory, provided the foot that contacted fair territory made contact before the foot in foul territory. If both feet, one in foul and one in fair territory, contact the ground simultaneously, the pass is considered complete.

Section 3   The ball shall be put in play within 25 seconds after it is declared ready for play, unless time is suspended during that period.

PENALTY: 5 yards (Rule 5, Section 3)

OFFICIAL HAND SIGNALS:
   DELAY OF GAME   BALL DEAD   BALL READY FOR PLAY

Rule 6. Series of Downs and Zone to Gain

Section 1   After each touchdown, the ball is put in play on the 20-yard line of the team just scored upon.

Section 2   The team in possession of the ball shall have 4 consecutive downs to advance to the next zone of scrimmage. Any down may be repeated if provided for by the rules.

Section 3   The line to gain in any series shall be the zone line in advance of the ball. If distance has been lost due to penalty or failure to gain, the original zone line in advance of the ball at the beginning of the series of downs is the line to gain. The most forward point of the ball, when declared dead between the goal lines, shall be the determining factor.

Section 4   A new series of downs shall be awarded when:

A.   A team moves the ball into the next zone on a play free from penalty.
B.   A penalty against the opponents moves the ball into the next zone.
C.   The opponents have obtained legal possession of a ball as a result of a touchdown, a free kick, kick from scrimmage, touchback, pass interception, pass interference, or failure to gain the zone in advance of the ball.

Section 5   If a penalty is declined, the number of the next down shall be whatever it would have been had the foul not occurred.

Section 6   The down is replayed on offsetting penalties.

Rule 7. Kicks

Section 1   A free kick begins play following a safety, whereby the ball shall be put in play by a placekick or a punt from some spot on or behind the quarter line of the team just scored upon.

Section 2   When the ball is legally kicked, all players of the kicking team must be inbounds and all players, except the holder and kicker of a placekick, must be behind their restraining line. At least 3 players of the receiving team must be within 5 yards of their restraining line (center line) until the ball is kicked.

Section 3   Any kick that hits the ground is dead at the spot.

Section 4   Any ball kicked out-of-bounds between an opponent's goal line and the 20-yard line will be put in play on the 20-yard line. Any ball kicked out-of-bounds at any other point will be put in play at the spot where it crossed the sideline.

Section 5   Any kick that becomes dead behind the goal or end line will be put in play on the 20-yard line.

Section 6   If a team is going to punt, it must inform the defensive team. After declaring it will punt, the offensive team as well as the defensive team must have 3 players on the line of scrimmage, and they must be down on one knee.

Rule 8.   Scrimmage, Snapping, Handing, and Passing the Ball

Section 1   The offensive team must be behind the line of scrimmage until the ball is centered, and the defensive team must be on their side of the scrimmage line when the ball is centered.

Section 2   All plays from scrimmage must be started by a legal snap from a point on the inbound line located midway between the sidelines.

Section 3   All offensive players must be within 15 yards of the ball and must be inbounds when it is snapped.

Section 4   No player of the offensive team shall make a false start.

Section 5   The offensive team shall have no more than 1 player in motion at a time prior to the snap. All players not in motion must come to a set position and hold that position at least 1 full second prior to the snap. (Violation of this rule is termed an illegal shift.)

Section 6   No offensive player, while on the scrimmage line, may receive a snap.

PENALTY: 5 yards (Rule 8, Sections 1-6)
OFFICIAL HAND SIGNAL: ILLEGAL PROCEDURE

Section 7   A ball carrier may not hand the ball forward except when behind his/her own scrimmage line when handing to a backfield teammate who is also behind the line.

PENALTY: 5 yards (Rule 8, Section 7)

OFFICIAL HAND SIGNAL: ILLEGAL HANDING BALL FORWARD

Section 8   A ball carrier may pass the ball backward at any time. A backward pass or fumble may be caught in flight inbounds by any player and advanced.

Section 9   All players are eligible to receive a forward pass.

Section 10   A forward pass is illegal:

A. If the passer is beyond the line of scrimmage when the ball leaves his/her hand.
B. If more than 1 forward pass is made from behind the line of scrimmage.
C. If intentionally thrown to ground or out-of-bounds.

PENATY: 5 yards and loss of down (Rule 8, Section 10)
HAND SIGNAL:
    ILLEGAL FORWARD PASS   INTENTIONAL GROUNDING

Section 11   Contact by an opponent that interferes with an eligible player who is beyond the line of scrimmage is pass interference. Some contact is legal if it is made before the ball is thrown or if opposing players are simultaneously attempting to catch the ball.

PENALTY: Offensive interference—15 yards and loss of down. Defensive interference—first down at the spot of the foul; if in the end zone, first down at the 1-yard line.
HAND SIGNAL: PASS INTERFERENCE

Rule 9. Conduct of Players and Others Subject to the Rules

Section 1   Whenever, in the judgment of any game official, the following acts are deliberate or flagrant, the players involved shall be suspended from the game:

A. Using fist, kicking, or kneeing.
B. Using locked hands, elbows, or any part of the forearm or hand, except according to rules.
C. Tackling the ball carrier as in regulation football.
D. Any other deliberate or flagrant act.

Section 2   There shall be no unsportsmanlike conduct by players, substitutes, coaches, or others subject to the rules, including:

A. Abusive or insulting language.
B. Any acts of unfair play.
C. Managers, coaches, or others on the field of play at any time without permission, or their interference of any nature with the progress of the game.
D. Players leaving the field of play other than during the intermission at halftime.
E. A substitute or any other person interfering with a player or play while the ball is alive.
F. Using a "hideout play" by placing a player or players near the sideline who were not within 15 yards of the ball at the ready-for-play signal.
G. The punter delaying his kick after requesting protection.
H. Attempting to substitute a suspended player.
I. A defensive player pulling or removing a flag from an offensive player as the ball is snapped or during a play with the obvious intent of making the offensive player ineligible to become a pass receiver or a ball carrier.

PENALTY: 15 yards, and if flagrant, offender shall be disqualified.
OFFICIAL HAND SIGNAL:

Section 3   The referee may enforce any penalty considered equitable, including the awarding of a score, in the following situations:

A. If a team refuses to play within 2 minutes after ordered to play by the referee.
B. If play is interfered with by an obviously unfair or unsportsmanlike act not specifically covered by the rules.

C. If a team repeatedly commits fouls that can be penalized only by halving the distance to its goal line.

For refusal to play or for repeated fouls, the referee shall, after warning, forfeit the game to the opponents.

Section 4   No player shall commit a personal foul during any period of play or intermission. Any act prohibited hereunder or any other act of unnecessary roughness is a personal foul.

A. There shall be no contact with an opponent who is on the ground.
B. There shall be no tripping, clipping, or hurdling.
C. The runner shall not be thrown to the ground.
D. There shall be no unnecessary roughness of any nature.

E. The ball carrier shall not deliberately drive or run into a defensive player. (Violation of this rule is called offensive charging.)

PENALTY: 15 yards. Flagrant offenders may be disqualified.
OFFICIAL HAND SIGNAL: PERSONAL FOUL

Section 5   The offensive team shall be prohibited from obstructing an opponent with extended hand or arm. This includes the use of a "stiff arm" extended to ward off an opponent.

Section 6   The ball carrier shall not protect his/her flags by blocking (with the arms or hands) the opportunity of an opponent to pull or remove a flag.

Section 7   The defensive player shall not hold, grasp, or obstruct forward progress of a ball carrier when in the act of removing a flag.

Section 8   Defensive players may not use their hands to grasp, push, or pull an opponent in an attempt to get at the ball carrier.

PENALTY: 15 yards from spot of foul (Rule 9, Sections 5-8)
OFFICIAL HAND SIGNAL: ILLEGAL USE OF HANDS

Section 9   While a pass is in flight, any player may bat the ball in any direction. No players shall bat any other free ball in flight forward in the field of play, or in any direction if it is in an end zone.

PENALTY: 5 yards from spot of foul.
OFFICIAL HAND SIGNAL: ILLEGAL BATTING

Section 10   The terms *blocking* and *screening* are synonymous terms in REC Football and shall be executed by body position alone and without body contact. It is recommended that the offensive player setting up the block or screen interlock his/her hands behind the back. Two types of fouls may result from enforcement of this rule.

A. An offensive player is guilty of illegal blocking if he/she in any way initiates contact with a defensive player who has established a path to the ball carrier. The player screening or blocking must move his/her body in such a manner as to cause the defensive player to travel the greatest distance to down the ball carrier.

PENALTY: 10 yards from previous spot.
OFFICIAL HAND SIGNAL: ILLEGAL BLOCKING

B. Defensive players are guilty of defensive charging if, in attempting to down the ball carrier, they charge over or use their hand on a defensive player in order to get to the ball carrier. An offensive player who established a position cannot be run over.

PENALTY: 10 yards from spot of foul.
OFFICIAL HAND SIGNAL: DEFENSIVE CHARGING

Rule 10. Enforcement of Penalties

Section 1 A penalty is completed when it is accepted, declined, or cancelled according to rule. Any penalty may be declined, but a disqualified player must leave the game.

Section 2 When a foul is committed at a time other than following a touchdown and before the ball is ready for play on a conversion, the penalty shall be completed before the ball is declared ready for play for any ensuing down. A penalty incurred after a touchdown and before the ball is ready for play for the conversion, shall be completed on the ensuing series of plays from the 20-yard line. A foul by the defense during a successful conversion is enforced on the ensuing series of plays from the 20-yard line.

Section 3 A foul that occurs simultaneously with a snap or free kick is penalized from the spot of the snap or free kick.

Section 4 When two or more fouls by the same team are reported to the referee before the penalty for any one of them has been completed, the referee shall explain the alternative penalties to the field captain of the offended team, who may then elect only one of these penalties.

Section 5 If fouls by both teams are reported to the referee before the penalty for any one of them has been completed, each such foul is an offsetting foul, the penalties cancel each other, and the down is replayed. Exception: When team possession changes during a down and either team had committed a foul prior to possession, the down is not replayed and the penalty is enforced against the team that elects to retain the ball.

Section 6 The basic enforcement spots are: the previous spot, the spot of the foul, and the succeeding spot.

Section 7 Specified enforcement spot includes:

A. The enforcement spot for a foul committed when the ball is dead is the succeeding spot; except when the foul occurred after a touchdown and before the ball is ready for play for the conversion, the enforcement would be on the ensuing series of plays from the 20-yard line.
B. Ordinarily, the enforcement spot is the spot specified in the penalty. Exception to this is that no distance penalty shall exceed half the distance to the goal line.

Section 8 When no enforcement spot is specified, or when the time of the foul is as stated below, enforcement shall be as follows:

A. If the ball was in possession, enforcement shall be from the spot of the foul with the following exceptions:
    1. If the foul occurs prior to an incomplete legal forward pass or against the passer during a complete legal forward pass, enforcement is from the previous spot.
    2. If a foul is behind the goal line of the offended team, enforcement shall be from that goal line.
    3. Enforcement for a foul by the defense (except as stated in 1. above) committed behind its goal line shall be: opponent's ball, first down, on

the offender's 1-yard line, or half-way between the previous spot and that goal line if the previous spot was on or inside the 1-yard line.

4. If the foul occurs during a successful conversion, a team may elect the enforcement spot of the penalty from the spot of the ensuing series of plays from the 20-yard line.

B. If the ball was free, enforcement shall be as follows:

1. From a free kick or a scrimmage kick that did not cross the restraining line or line of scrimmage and had touched a member of the kicking team, the ball shall be awarded to the receiving team at the spot the ball was touched.

2. From a free kick or a scrimmage kick that had crossed the restraining line or line of scrimmage and the receiving team commits a foul before it had touched a receiving team player, the penalty will be assessed from the previous spot, with the kicking team retaining possession.

Can you demonstrate the official's hand signals for the following situations: ball ready for play; ball dead; touchdown; safety; and illegal procedure?

Rule 11. Coed REC Football Rules

In adapting official REC Football rules for use in Coed REC Football, the object has been to keep as close to the original rules as possible and at the same time to eliminate the dangers of body contact.

Section 1 The rules pertaining to the playing field, player's equipment, length of game, time-outs, yardage and downs, method of downing the ball carrier, fumbles, punts, substitutions, scoring, etc. shall be the same as those for Official REC Football. Coed REC Football will be conducted with the following exceptions.

Section 2 The number of players shall be 6, 3 of whom must be female. Six players must be present to start a game.

Section 3

A. Advancement from behind the line of scrimmage to beyond the line of scrimmage is restricted to females only. A male cannot carry the ball across the line of scrimmage under any circumstances. There are no advancement limitations on a male once he has obtained possession beyond the line of scrimmage.

B. A male or female may execute any number of laterals to receivers of either sex behind the line of scrimmage, but only females may advance the ball across the line of scrimmage.

C. A male cannot advance a kick forward from his point of contact with the ball, but may move backwards or laterally from that first point of contact. Advancement via a kick is only possible by a female ball carrier. (Usually the male catches the ball and then laterals off to a female.)

D. If the passer is female, she can complete her passes to either sex, but if completed to a male, he must be beyond the line of scrimmage at the time of the reception. If the passer is a male, he can complete his pass to a female anywhere on the field. One male-to-male beyond the line of scrimmage attempt is allowed every set of 4 downs.

SUMMARY OF PENALTIES

Loss of Down

Illegally handing ball forward (also loss of 5 yards)
Illegal forward pass (also loss of 5 yards)
Intentionally grounding pass (also loss of 5 yards)
Offensive pass interference (also loss of 15 yards)

Loss of 5 Yards

Excess time-out illegally used or requested
Illegal delay of the game
Putting ball in play before declared ready-for-play
Infraction of free kick formation
Illegal snap
Infraction of scrimmage formation
Interference with opponents or the ball
False start or simulating start of a play
Player on line receiving snap
Illegally handing ball forward (also loss of down)
Intentionally grounding pass (also loss of down)
Illegal kick
Illegal shift

Loss of 10 Yards

Illegal blocking
Defensive charging

Loss of 15 Yards

Team not ready to play at start of either half
Interference with opportunity to catch a kick
Offensive pass interference (also loss of down)
Forward pass illegally touched (also loss of down)
Striking, kicking, kneeing, elbowing, etc.
Unsportsmanlike conduct
Infraction of rules during intermission
Persons illegally on the field
Hurdling
Tripping
Clipping
Illegal use of hand or arm by offense
Illegal use of hand or arm by defense

Protecting flags
Offensive charging by ball carrier

Offended Team's Ball At Spot of Foul

Short free kick illegally touched by kicking team
Illegally touching free kick after being out-of-bounds
Defensive pass interference
Illegal use of hand or arm when ball is free
Illegally batting free ball
Illegally kicking or kicking at a free ball
Other fouls when the ball is free
Illegal touching of scrimmage kick

After receiving a lateral pass from a female, a male player advances the ball from behind the line of scrimmage by carrying the ball across the line. What is the official's decision?

OFFICIATING

No team sport game can be enjoyable or functional without good officiating, and such is the case in REC Football. For this reason a systematic method of training officials, such as a class or clinic, is absolutely necessary. Pertinent areas that should be covered include mechanics, rules, first aid, responsibilities, jurisdictions, and philosophy of officiating. It may also include practice games, problem sessions, assignment sessions, films, and guest speakers. Keep in mind that a REC Football program is only as good as its officials.

It is suggested that a minimum of two officials and a maximum of three officials be used for REC Football for physical education classes, intramurals, and other recreational programs. The responsibilities of each of these officials are as follows:

Every official should have a knowledge of:

1. The rules.
2. The mechanics of officiating the position for which responsible.
3. The proper use of the whistle.
4. The proper use of the penalty flags.
5. All options and enforcement spots.
6. How to mark dead ball spots.
7. Proper hand signals.
8. Temporary first aid methods.

The *head referee* shall:

1. Give the proper option to the team captains.
2. Perform pregame procedures.
3. Keep the 25-second count.

4. Keep up with time-outs taken.
5. Be sure that the score (including 20-yard penetrations) is kept correctly.
6. Take a position behind and to the right or left of the offensive backfield (fig. 3.2).
7. Be responsible for the following areas:
   a. The offensive backfield
   b. Protection of the quarterback
   c. Interline play
8. After the play has progressed up field, follow, watching for fouls occurring behind the ball carrier.
9. Be responsible for spotting the ball after each play.

The umpire shall:

1. Keep official time.
2. Be responsible for player equipment.
3. Spot the down marker after each play.
4. In the case of only two officials, keep official score.

Figure 3.2

5. Take a position on the line of scrimmage when two officials are working, and behind the defensive backfield when three officials are working.
6. Be responsible for the following areas:
    a. Offsides when only two officials are working
    b. Interline play
    c. Pass patterns and pass interference
    d. The sideline opposite the down marker

The *lineman* shall:

1. Keep official score.
2. Spot the down marker following every play.
3. Be responsible for the game ball and flags.
4. Be responsible for the following areas:
    a. Offsides when three officials are working
    b. Interline play
    c. The sideline adjacent to the down marker

The *downsmarker holder* shall:

1. Be furnished by each of the teams.
2. Serve in this capacity for half of the game.
3. Operate the downsmarker according to the umpire's instructions.

Do you know which official is responsible for each of the following duties: keeping the official score; performing pregame procedures; keeping the official time; keeping the 25 second count?

Figure 3.3 shows the proper position for a three-man team of officials. Notice the triangle that the three officials form. A team of officials should keep the area of this triangle as large as possible at all times.

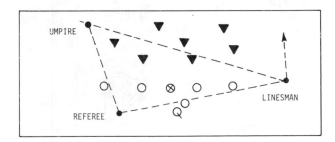

Figure 3.3

OFFICIALS' SIGNALS

ILLEGALLY PASSING
OR HANDING BALL
FORWARD

INTENTIONAL
GROUNDING

ILLEGAL USE OF
HANDS AND ARMS

PERSONAL FOUL

NON-CONTACT FOULS

FORWARD PASS OR
KICK CATCHING
INTERFERENCE

PLAYER DISQUALIFIED

BALL ILLEGALLY
TOUCHED, KICKED,
OR BATTED

CLIPPING

ILLEGAL BLOCKING

OFFENSIVE CHARGING

DEFENSIVE CHARGING

OFFICIALS' SIGNALS

BALL READY FOR PLAY	BALL DEAD; IF HAND IS MOVED FROM SIDE TO SIDE: TOUCHBACK	TIME OUT
FIRST DOWN	TOUCHDOWN OR CONVERSION	SAFETY
OFFSIDE	INCOMPLETE FORWARD PASS, PENALTY DECLINED, NO PLAY, OR NO SCORE	DELAY OF GAME
ILLEGAL PROCEDURE OR POSITION	ILLEGAL MOTION	ILLEGAL SHIFT

organization for play and strategy
4

There are three main areas of strategy: personnel placement, offensive strategy, and defensive strategy. REC Football rules utilize a 7-man team since this is the most popular size team. Seventy-five percent of the intramural programs in the United States use 7-man rules for flag and touch football.

To give some insight into the reason 7-man rules are used most often, let us look at the game. Due to the restricted size of playing areas, confusion and congestion arise with teams numbering 9 or 11. Congestion provides opportunity for accidental collisions, thus increasing the chances of injury. When playing 7-man football, the number of eligible receivers closely resembles that of regulation football; therefore, many well-known strategies, both offensive and defensive, can be applied to the game. Also, it is easier to find 14 people to play than it is to find 18 or 22, thus increasing the number of teams and allowing a higher participation level whether it be elementary, high school, college, or community recreation football.

PERSONNEL PLACEMENT

Flag and touch football are games of skill and finesse, not games of strength. For this reason, fleet, quick, and agile players usually are the better performers. The type of strategy and organization a team may use are by far the most important part of the game. However, REC Football is a recreational game and no person should be overlooked. For this reason, it is suggested that no person play both offense and defense.

The first thing a coach needs to do is draw up a personnel chart, listing each person, his/her better attributes, and previous experience. In determining a player's skill level, any of the skill tests included in chapter 6 may be used. Before positioning individual players, let us look at the normal offensive and defensive sets. Offensively, 7-man football has two ends, two guards, one center, one quarterback, and one halfback. Defensively, there are two safeties, two cornerbacks, two rushers, and one middle linebacker. The basic set is illustrated in figure 4.1.

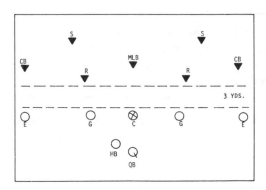

Figure 4.1

Recreational football, with its lack of blocking, is basically a passing game; therefore, the offense should be designed around the pass. Every team must have a quarterback who can throw fairly proficiently and a center who is very agile and who can make a good deep snap with regularity. Halfbacks must be both good runners and good receivers. It is also good if the halfback can pass fairly well. The ends must have good speed and good moves, but most of all they must have good hands. The guards must be quick in order to screen block, but since they are also eligible receivers, their pass receiving ability must not be sold short. It is also advantageous for the guards to be tall to allow for a larger physical screen.

When two good teams meet, the better defensive team usually wins. It has been said, "The best defense is a good offense," but there are so many factors in favor of the defense, such as blocking and the field size, that this statement should probably be reversed for REC Football.

Defensive personnel placement is very critical. First, a team must have two rushers who are quick, agile, and preferably tall, in order to avoid screeners as well as to affect the passer with upraised arms. The two cornerbacks must be quick and must have good speed in order to cover a receiver in a man-to-man defense. The cornerbacks must also have good touch or flag pulling technique. The two safeties must have good speed, but not necessarily as good as the cornerbacks because they have more of a cushion with which to work. Also, in a zone defense they play outfield-type positions and have more time to go to the ball. The middle linebacker needs to be the best all-around athlete on the team, with good rushing ability, good speed, and good touch or flag pulling technique. But, most of all, the middle linebacker is the defensive leader and must be able to read plays as pass or run and make adjustments accordingly.

The punter and placekicker do not need to have great distances but must be very accurate. Runbacks can be costly and must be eliminated. Punts should be kicked into the end zone or out-of-bounds inside the 20-yard line. In both cases, the ball is placed on the 20-yard line, which means that the offensive team must move the ball an entire zone to get a first down.

No matter what the overall skill level of a team may be, a coach needs to be very careful in placing the players so that everyone is placed where he/she will do the team the most good. It may take a couple of games before personnel

Assume you are lining up a defensive team. Among your players are several with special abilities. In which positions will you place each player? A—the best all-around athlete; B—has good speed and quick reactions; C—is an accurate kicker; D—is tall, speedy, and agile?

finally becomes situated, but it should be remembered that an organized team with fair athletes will usually beat an unorganized team with good athletes.

OFFENSIVE STRATEGY

REC Football is basically a passing game. Due to the zone defenses used by most teams, the emphasis is on the short passing game. Just as the run is used to set up the pass in regulation football, the short pass is used to set up the run as well as the long pass.

Every offensive play should be designed to take advantage of weaknesses in a particular defense. Thus, every play called in the huddle should have some logic or reasoning behind it. To function properly, an offensive team must be organized. Every time a play is called, the quarterback must do three things: call the formation, call the play, and give the snap count. All of this information- must be given quickly and distinctly: for instance, "spread formation, 45 pass left, on two." Without this type of organization in the huddle, a team will be invariably called for delay of game.

Most teams use three basic formations: normal, spread, and slot (fig. 4.2). All of these are designed to spread or cause a defense to make some kind of adjustment and should be used accordingly.

There are many pass patterns, as shown in figures 4.3 and 4.4, and all have their particular advantages. Also, certain combinations can make some patterns even more advantageous against certain defenses. It is suggested that all offensive players know the names of each pattern.

Figure 4.5 illustrates an example of a short or deep pass play from the normal formation. The quarterback has indicated the formation, the play, and the

Figure 4.2

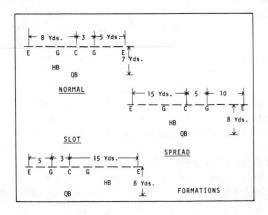

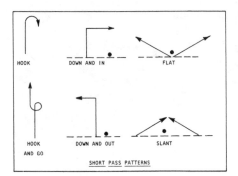

Figure 4.3

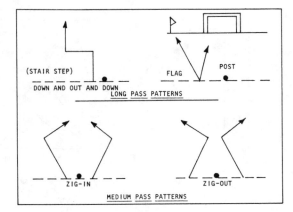

Figure 4.4

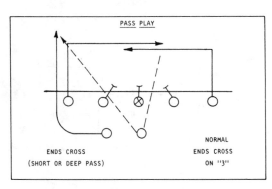

Figure 4.5

snap count by calling "normal, ends cross, on 3." An example of a pass play from the *slot* formation is illustrated in figure 4.6. This play is good for short yardage and may be executed to either the left or right side.

The most frequently used method to beat a zone defense is to flood zones. The most frequently used tactic to beat a man-to-man defense is to isolate on a weak defender, as well as to run occasionally in order to set up long passes. Plays are designed to be executed against certain defenses and in certain situations. Suggested plays are illustrated in the figure 4.7.

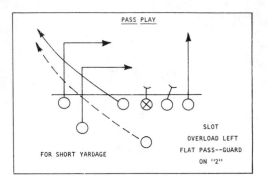

Figure 4.6

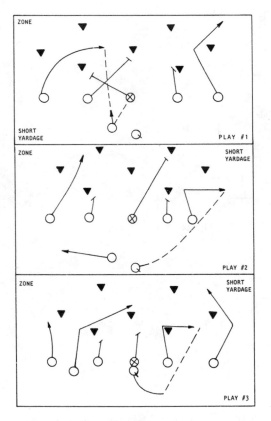

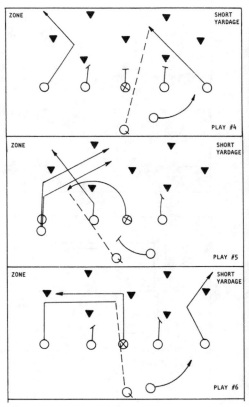

Figure 4.7 (Plays #1—32)

Figure 4.7. Cont'd.

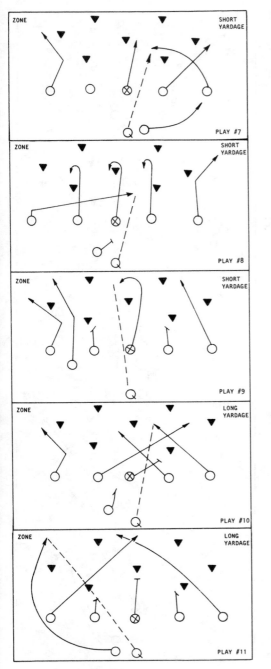

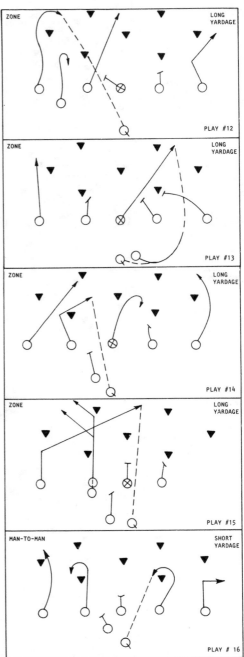

Figure 4.7. Cont'd.

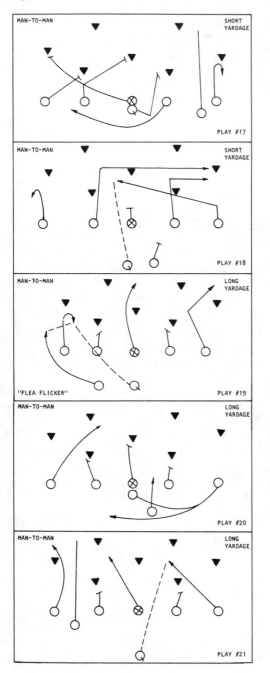

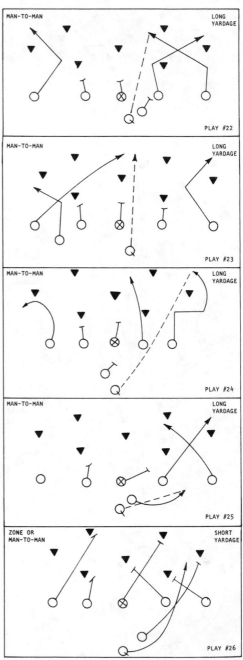

Figure 4.7. Cont'd.

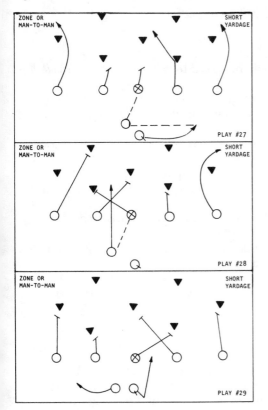

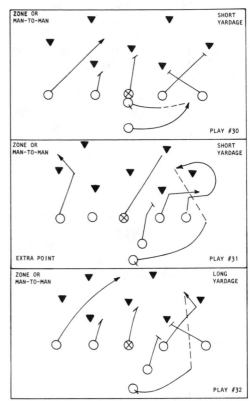

Offensive Tips

1. Prior to the game, a good team always learns as much about the opponent's defense as possible.
2. Offensive players should take the same stance each play so as to not give away the intent of the play.
3. If a defensive player seems to be tiring, run plays at him/her and take advantage of his/her weakness.
4. A defense that is shifting around prior to the snap can be caught off guard with plays run on quick counts.
5. Every defense has basic strengths and weaknesses, and plays should be designed to take advantage of them.
6. When possessing the ball inside your own 20-yard line, play selection should be conservative to help avoid costly errors.
7. Second and short yardage is an ideal situation to waste a play and go for a touchdown.

8. Don't consistently run toward the wide side of the field.
9. Motion, flankers, and widening your formation are good tactics to distract a stunting or stacked defense.
10. Always vary your snap count to keep the defense guessing.
11. Try to establish the plays that work best for you early in the game.
12. Third-down plays should be designed and called to gain first-down yardage only.
13. Your passing game should not be designed for only one receiver.
14. A long pass intercepted deep in a team's own territory can serve the same purpose as a "coffin corner" punt.
15. Passes thrown on first down are more likely to be successful than those thrown on third down.
16. If you find yourself behind early, don't abandon your game plan to get even quickly. Stay calm and stay with the "bread-and-butter" part of your game.
17. When ahead late in a game, abandon your passing game for the conservative running game.
18. When behind late in a game, use short- and medium-length passes. The defense will be set to stop the long pass.
19. The long pass on the first play of a game can swing momentum your way.
20. Yardage and field position gained by kicking is just as valuable as that gained by other offensive means.

DEFENSIVE STRATEGY

Defense is one of the more crucial aspects of the game. There are basically two types of defense: man-to-man and zone. There are several variations in relation to either type, but most teams run one of these types or an alternation of the two.

Man-to-Man Defense

A man-to-man defense is just what it implies: every man is responsible for a predesignated player on every play. The defensive responsibilities are shown in figure 4.8.

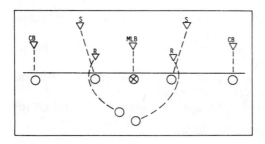

Figure 4.8

The rushers take a hard outside rush trying to keep the quarterback contained, forcing a pass. The halfback is the rusher's responsibility, to whose side the halfback lines up while the other rusher is responsible for the quarterback. The cornerbacks cover the ends no matter where they go. The safeties are responsible for the guards. If the guards stay in to block, the safeties will help the cornerbacks on deep coverage as well as pick up the halfback coming out of the backfield to their side. Once again, the middle linebacker is a key position for reading the play as pass or run and notifying one's team. If it is a run the middle linebacker goes with the flow of the play. In man-to-man coverage, in the case of a pass, the center is the main responsibility of the middle linebacker. If the center stays in to block, the center linebacker drops and slides in the direction that needs coverage, always looking for a possible fake and run.

A good offense will locate a mismatch in a man-to-man defense and work on it. For this reason, it is probably best to run a basic zone, bringing in a man-to-man defense every third or fourth play, or as needed to keep the offense honest. However, the key to every defense is for all players to know their responsibility on every play. Just as much practice should go into defensive as into offensive preparation.

2-3-2 Zone Defense

Figure 4.9 shows the basic areas of responsibility for each defensive position. The zone defense is designed to stop the long pass and hold the run to short yardage. It also allows for more interceptions because all players are free to go for the ball, and double coverage occurs on some occasions. As illustrated, the two rushers take a hard outside rush, being sure to contain the passer. The cornerbacks cover the ends or whichever receiver first enters their zone, and continues coverage until that receiver leaves their zone or until another receiver enters that zone. If a receiver enters the zone closer to the line of scrimmage, the cornerback releases the deeper receiver to the safety and begins coverage on the shorter receiver. Even if no receiver enters a cornerback's zone, he/she stays in the zone expecting a reverse or throwback type of pass. The safety men key the ends while scanning to pick up a receiver coming toward their zone. Once

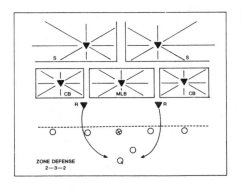

Figure 4.9

a receiver penetrates the safety's zone, that receiver is the safety's responsibility no matter how deep the receiver goes. Cornerbacks have receivers in their zone almost immediately, and therefore must play the man. However, the safety men have enough time before a receiver reaches their zone to read the play as a pass or run by the quarterback's action.

If the play is read as a running play, the cornerback cautiously begins to react in order to contain the runner while shouting "run" so as to notify any players who may have their back to the ball that it is a running play. The cornerback helps on short coverage if no receiver enters his/her zone. If two receivers enter the zone, the word two is shouted, thus notifying the defense man who does not have a receiver to cover that help is needed. In the case of two receivers, the safety always covers the deepest pattern.

The middle linebacker is the key person in every defense. When the ball is snapped, this linebacker must make an immediate judgment as to whether it is a passing or a running play. If the play is a run, the middle linebacker must shout "run" and close in on the ball carrier, being sure to contain the runner so as to hold the yardage gained to a minimum. If the play is read as a pass, this linebacker drops back in the direction where help is needed on coverage. Middle linebackers never turn their backs to the quarterback, and their area of coverage is always that area from approximately 5 yards on either side of the ball and 7-10 yards deep.

2-2-3 Zone Defense

This zone defense (fig. 4.10) should be used when either you have slow cornerbacks or the opposition is running a lot of option plays. The cornerbacks key the ends; if they go down and in, they release; if they go down and out, they take them all the way, even if they turn and go deep. If they see an option play coming, they take the quarterback all the way; if it is away from them, they drop and flow with the play. The two strong safety men key the ends also; if they come down and in, they pick them up until the free safety takes over. If they go down and out, they look for the next receiver to enter their zone. If an option play comes their way, the pitchman is theirs. The free safety is just that: free to roam and go to the ball. He/she will always drop deeper as the play expands unless he/she has read "run" and is going to the ball.

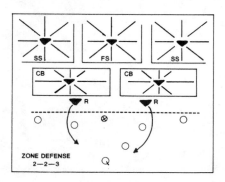

Figure 4.10

A zone defense will stop the long pass and the run, but by flooding zones, an offensive team can pick away yardage of 5-10 yards per play until they score. When a team uses these tactics, shifting to a man-to-man defense is advisable.

Defensive Tips

1. Defensive strategy should not only be designed to stop the opponent but also to gain possession and field position and to score by punt return or interception.
2. Before setting the defense for each play, the down, score, field position, and offensive tendencies should be considered.
3. Every team should have a variety of defenses to use and should mix them to keep the offense off balance.
4. Each defense should be able to adjust for shifts, motion, or other variations used to throw off offensive strategy.
5. Defensive linemen should always give a hard rush but should keep under control to avoid being trapped.
6. Defensive backs should play the receiver first and then the ball once it has been thrown.
7. Defensive backs should never let a receiver behind them.
8. A good pass rush will eliminate a high completion rate on long passes due to lack of time.
9. Defensive linemen should communicate prior to every snap so that costly mistakes are not made.
10. Man-to-man defenses should be used sparingly because they tire your personnel.
11. Zone defenses allow for more interceptions.
12. Man-to-man defenses allow your best defensive back to cover the opponent's best receiver.
13. Man-to-man pass defense eliminates most coverage mistakes.
14. Prior to returning a punt, a decision should be made as to which direction it will be returned.
15. Defensive players should try to pick up keys from offensive alignment.
16. The more you know about your opponent the better you can defense them.
17. Don't gamble with stunts when a team is inside your 20-yard line.
18. Watch for long or trick plays on second down and short yardage.
19. Always turn a play back into the inside where you have help.
20. When ahead late in a game, use a deep zone defense to avoid giving up a long, quick touchdown.

When your team is defending, what kind of play by the offense might be anticipated under each of these circumstances? A—offensive team is ahead late in the game; B—it is second down with short yardage; C—it is 3rd down.

---

drills
5

The fundamental skills of REC Football may be learned and developed effectively and pleasurably through a variety of practice activities. Your personal enjoyment is largely dependent upon your ability to perform the individual skills that comprise the game. Challenging and meaningful drills that allow you to practice using the correct technique will be of great benefit, since perfection is best attained through repetition of properly executed skills.

A variety of drills is presented in this chapter, while chapter 6 includes skill tests that may be practiced as drills or adapted for squad competition. You may choose to perform many of the drills as relays, since competition puts more pressure on you to perform with greater precision.

KEY TO DIAGRAMS:

SPIRAL TOSS

Skills

Grip and spiral release.

Formation

Scattered.

Description

1. The player assumes the proper grip on the football with the hand at waist level and the palm up.
2. The ball hand is lowered from waist level to an extended arm position near the thigh and the ball is tossed to self directly overhead with a high follow-through of the hand.
3. If executed properly, the ball will spiral and the player tossing the ball will be able to catch it without taking a step.
4. This drill should be repeated until the player is consistently successful at spiraling the ball to self.

Variations

1. Close the eyes while tossing the ball, open them in time to see if the ball is spiraling.
2. Execute the toss with the nondominant hand.

STATIONARY PASSING

Skills

Forward pass and receiving a passed ball.

Formation

Double Lines   Staggered Lines

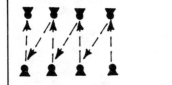   

Description

1. The players face each other in parallel lines—either directly opposite or staggered, approximately 5 yards apart.
2. The ball is passed from one player to another so that it travels from one end of the information to the other, zigzag fashion.
3. The ball may be passed from the last person directly to the lead person or it may be passed back up the line, zigzag fashion.

Variations

1. Increase the distance as the skill level improves.
2. Shorten the distance for the flat pass; use longer distances for the lob or floater.

SHUTTLE PASSING

Skills

Forward pass and receiving a passed ball.

Formation

Shuttle   *File-Leader*

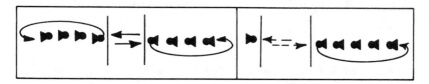

Description

1. The players assume file formations, 5-10 yards apart.
2. The ball is passed back and forth between the two parts of the shuttle.
3. The player goes to the end of his/her own line after taking a turn.
4. In the file-leader formation, a new leader may be used after one or two complete rotations of the file.

Variations

1. Increase the distance as the skill level improves.
2. Allow the leader in the file-leader formation to remain in position until he/she misses the ball or throws a poor pass.

RUN AND PASS BACK

Skills

Passing (forward pass, lateral, center), receiving a passed ball, and ball carrying.

Formation

File

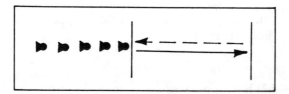

Description

1. The first player runs with the ball to the turning line, a distance of 20-25 feet.
2. The player turns around and throws a forward pass to the next player in line.
3. This procedure is repeated until the last player in the line catches the ball and runs across the turning line.

Variations

1. Shorten the distance between the lines to 10-12 feet and center the ball instead of using the forward pass.
2. Shorten the distance between the lines to 8-10 feet and lateral the ball.
3. For the forward pass drill, place obstacles for the player to run in and out of on the way to the turning line.

DOUBLE-LINE CENTERING

Skills

Centering, receiving, and passing.

Formation

Double Lines   Staggered Lines

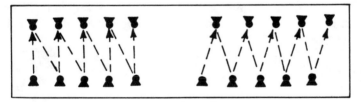

Description

1. The players are in parallel lines—either directly opposite or staggered, facing the same direction 10-12 feet apart.
2. The ball is centered from one player to another so that the ball travels from one end of the formation to the other in zigzag formation.
3. The ball may be passed from the last person directly to the lead person or it may be centered back up the line in zigzag fashion.

Variations

1. Decrease the distance between the lines to 6-8 feet.
2. One line may center the ball, while the other line receives the center and passes across to the next player.

SHUTTLE CENTERING

Skills

Centering, receiving, and passing.

Formation

Shuttle   File-Leader

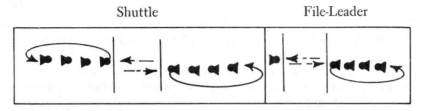

Description

1. The players assume file formations 10-12 feet apart.
2. The ball is centered back and forth between the two parts of the shuttle.
3. The player goes to the end of his/her own line after taking a turn.
4. In the file-leader formation, a new leader may be used after one or two complete rotations of the file.

Variations

1. Shuttle—the players forming one file may center the ball, while each player in the other file receives the ball and passes back to the person who will be the next center. Exchange centering and passing assignments after several complete rotations.
2. File-leader—players in the file center the ball, while the leader always receives the centered ball and passes back to the next player. Rotate leaders periodically.

CENTERING RELAY

Skills

Centering, receiving, lateraling, and ball carrying.

Formation

File

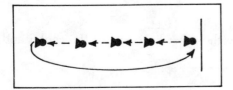

Description

1. All players face the front of the line 10-12 feet apart.
2. Each player centers the ball to the next in line, making sure the ball is placed on the ground prior to centering.
3. The last player in line runs to the front of the line with the ball.
4. Repeat until the team is back in its original position.

Variations

1. The direct snap type of centering may be used, necessitating that the players be closer together.
2. The lateral may be combined with this drill so that the first player centers the ball and the second player receives it, pivots, and laterals to the next player. Continue, alternating the center with the lateral, until the ball is received by the last player and carried to the head of the line.

CENTER AND PASS RELAY

Skills

Centering, running, forward pass, and receiving over shoulder.

Formation

File

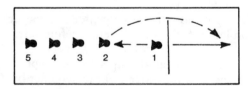

Description

1. Player #1 centers the ball to player #2, who is standing approximately 10-12 feet behind player #1.
2. Player #1 then runs downfield a designated distance (5 yards recommended), looks back, and, while running, receives a forward pass over the shoulder from player #2.
3. After catching or recovering the passed ball, #1 passes the ball back to #2 and goes to the end of the line.
4. Player #2 repeats the above with #3.
5. Continue until each player has had several tries.

Variation

1. Increase the passing distance according to the skill level of the players.

PASSING TO AN END

Skills

Centering, passing, receiving, and defending.

Formation

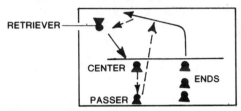

Description

1. The ball is centered to the passer, who is standing approximately 10-12 feet in back of the center.
2. As the ball is centered, the first end (lined up 3-5 yards from center) runs forward 5-10 yards, cuts to the inside, and receives a pass.
3. The end tosses the ball to the receiver, who takes the ball to the centering position.
4. Rotate after each pass: the retriever becomes the center, the center becomes the passer, the passer goes to the back of the line of ends, and the pass receiver becomes the new retriever.

Variations

1. Use the same formation as above, except have the end line up on the left side or alternate lining up on the right and left side.
2. Rather than rotating positions with each pass, the same center and passer work together for one or more complete rotations of the ends before selecting a new passer and center.
3. A defender, stationed in the pass receiving area, attempts to intercept or break up the pass. The end becomes the next defender and the defender becomes the retriever.

PASSING OPTION DRILL

Skills

Centering, passing, receiving, and defending.

Formation

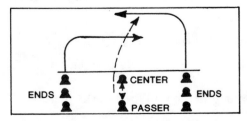

Description

1. Half of the ends line up to the right of the center and the other half line up to the left.
2. The ball is centered to the passer who is standing approximately 10-12 feet in back of the center.
3. As the ball is centered, the end at the head of each line runs out for a pass, the end from the right running deeper than the end from the left, before cutting inside.
4. As the ends cross, the passer throws to one of the ends.
5. The ball is relayed in and the ends rotate to opposite lines.
6. The same passer and center work together for at least one complete rotation of ends before a new passer and center are chosen.

Variations

1. One defender, stationed in the pass receiving area, attempts to intercept or break up the pass. To rotate, the end from the right becomes the next defender and the defender moves to the end of the line on the left side.
2. Two defenders are stationed in the pass receiving area. The defenders remain in this position for one complete rotation of the ends, then change positions.

HOT POTATO HANDOFF/LATERAL

Skills

Handing off, receiving a handoff, lateral passing, and receiving a lateral pass.

Formation

Circle

Description

1. Form a circle facing outward:
   a. extended arm touching the shoulder of the player on either side (handoff).
   b. finger tips do not touch those of the player on either side when the arms are extended (lateral).
2. The ball is passed around the circle using the handoff/lateral in correct form and as quickly as possible.

3. Move the ball clockwise as well as counterclockwise.

   NOTE: The facing outward position "forces" the individual to receive the ball, pivot, and hand off/lateral slightly to the rear in accordance with the rules.

Variations

1. The instructor may blow the whistle or give a verbal command to indicate a change of direction.
2. More than one ball may be used.
3. The distance between players may be increased (lateral).
4. The type of lateral to be used may be designated.

STATIONARY ZIGZAG HANDOFF/LATERAL

Skills

Handing off, receiving a handoff, lateral passing, and receiving a lateral pass.

Formation

Staggered Double File

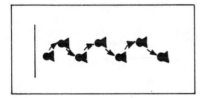

Description

1. Form two files facing the same direction and stagger positions so that the nearest player in the other file is not directly opposite.
   a. The players are very close together so that the handoff can be properly executed (handoff).
   b. The players are 6-10 feet apart (lateral).
2. The ball starts at the head of the double file and is handed off/lateralled across from one file to the other in zigzag fashion.
3. When the ball reaches the end, the players turn 180°, face the other direction, and repeat the drill.

   NOTE: This staggered position "forces" each person to execute the handoff/lateral to a player slightly behind him in accordance with the rules.

SHUTTLE HANDOFF

Skills

Handing off and receiving a handoff.

Formation

Shuttle

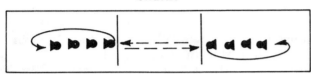

Description

1. Assume file formation, 5-10 yards apart.
2. The handoff is executed between the two players as they meet on the run.
3. The player goes to the end of the opposite line after executing the handoff.
   NOTE: The handoff should be made near the head of the receiver's line so that the receiver may carry the ball a short distance to prepare for the handoff to the oncoming player.

LATERAL PASSING DRILL

Skills

Lateral passing and receiving a lateral pass.

Formation

Double File

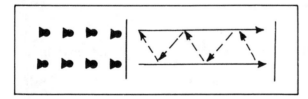

Description

1. The player with the ball runs parallel to a partner 6-10 feet away and laterals the ball to the partner.
2. The partner laterals back while both are running to the turning line 20 yards away.

NOTE: A lateral pass is defined as "a pass that is thrown sideways or back toward the passer's own goal." Thus, the passer and the receiver must constantly be changing their relative positions on the field.

3. When the turning line is reached, the players stop, turn around, and perform the drill on the return trip.
4. Each set of partners should attempt to complete at least 3 catches and 3 passes while traveling the 20 yards.

Variations

1. Upon reaching the turning line, the player with the ball stops, turns, and throws a forward pass back to the next partners waiting in line.
2. A shuttle formation may be used whereby the partners lateral for the 20 yards, hand off to the next couple, go to the end of that line, and wait for another turn.

PURSUIT DRILL

Skills

Ball carrying and flag pulling.

Formation

Parallel Lines

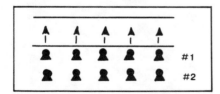

Description

1. All players are wearing flags and are standing at least 5-10 yards apart in each line.
2. The players in line #1 are ball carriers and stand approximately three steps ahead of the players in line #2.
3. On the signal "go," each player in line #2 chases the player directly in front in line #1 in an attempt to pull the flag.
4. Player #2 pursues the ball carrier until a flag is pulled or until the finish line is reached 50 yards away.
5. The runners should attempt to run fairly straight down the field within an imaginary 5-10-yard zone so as not to interfere with the runners on either side.
6. After a period of rest, the drill is performed from the finish line to the starting line with the #1s pursuing the #2s.

Variations

1. Vary the distance of the head start of the ball carriers.
2. Vary the distance of the pursuit itself.

ONE-ON-ONE DRILL

Skills

Ball carrying, dodging, and flag pulling.

Formation

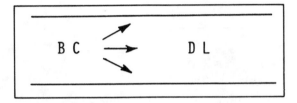

Description

1. One player is designated as the ball carrier (BC), the other as the defensive linesman (DL).
2. An area 5-10 yards in width and any designatetd length may be used.
3. On the signal "hike," the ball carrier attempts to maneuver past the defensive linesman.
4. The defensive linesman attempts to prevent the ball carrier from advancing the ball by pulling a flag.
5. The ball carrier may make any legal movement to get around the defensive linesman, such as fake, dodge, and change pace.

CONTAINMENT DRILL

Skills

Ball carrying, flag pulling, blocking, and screening.

Formation

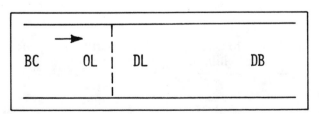

Description

1. The offensive players are ball carrier (BC) and offensive linesman (OL).
2. The defensive players are defensive linesman (DL) and defensive back (DB).
3. On the signal "hike," the defensive linesman rushes the ball carrier in an attempt to pull a flag.
4. The offensive linesman protects the ball carrier (who is theoretically looking for a pass receiver) by blocking (without contact).
5. If the offensive linesman is successful in forcing the rusher to the outside, the ball carrier runs with the ball.
6. During the run the offensive linesman may set up a screen for the ball carrier to prevent the defensive back from downing the runner after crossing the line of scrimmage.

FLAG PULLING

Skills

Passing, receiving, ball carrying, flag pulling, and pass defending.

Formation

File

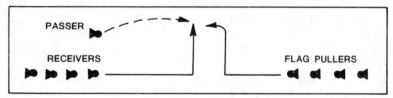

Description

1. The players line up in two files facing each other; one file of pass receivers, the other of flag pullers.
2. The receiver runs a short down-and-in pattern and receives the ball from the passer after the cut.
3. The flag puller defenses the receiver, allows the catch to be made, then attempts to pull both flags before the receiver has a chance to gain yardage.
4. The players rotate to the end of the opposite file.

Variation

1. The flag puller allows the receiver to catch the ball and start up field; then an attempt is made to pull the flags while trailing the receiver.

DEFENDING DRILL

Skills

Ball carrying, dodging, and flag pulling.

Formation

File

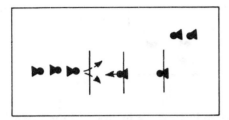

Description

1. The zone lines are 20 yards apart (official REC Football).
2. The ball carrier stands on the goal line ready to run.
3. Two defensive players, each stationed on a zone line facing the ball carrier, are responsible for the 20-yard zone immediately in front of their respective zone line.
4. When the ball carrier begins to run, the first defensive player moves into the first zone and attempts to down the ball carrier by pulling a flag.
5. The ball carrier runs, dodges, and tries to get by this defender and into the second zone.
6. If a flag is pulled, the ball carrier stops running and rotates to the defender line.
7. If a flag is not pulled by the first defensive player, the runner continues into the second zone.
8. When the ball carrier crosses the line into the second zone, the defender responsible for this zone leaves the line that he/she has been moving along (to stay in a strong defending position) and attempts to pull a flag of the runner.
9. After a completed run, the ball carrier rotates to the defender line and the defender rotates one position to the ball carrier line.

Variations

1. Allow the ball carrier to continue the run into the second zone even if a flag is pulled in the first zone.
2. The drill may be performed with a third defender in a third 20-yard zone.

BINGO DRILL

Skills

Pass defending and going for an interception.

Formation

File

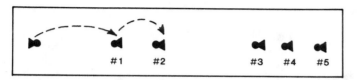

#1   #2   #3   #4   #5

Description

1. Form a single file; player #1 approximately 10 yards in front of the passer and player #2 about 3 yards behind #2.
2. The passer fakes a pass to the left and to the right.
3. Player # 1 reacts to the pass fakes.
4. The passer throws the ball slightly over the head of player #1, who tips the ball into the air and shouts "bingo."
5. Player #2, realizing that the ball is free, goes for the ball and attempts an interception.
6. The defenders rotate, i.e., #1 goes to the end of the line, #2 moves up into position to tip the pass, and #3 moves into position to attempt an interception.

KICKING DRILLS

Skills

Punting, placekicking, receiving a kicked ball, and return of kick.

Formation

Shuttle   Double Lines

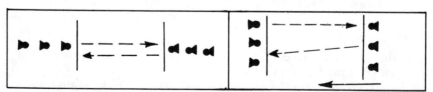

Description

1. The players are divided into two groups and assume a position on the field, kicking distance apart.
2. The players take turns kicking the ball back and forth across the kicking area, using either the punt or the placekick.
3. The players take turns catching the kicked balls.

   NOTE: The shuttle formation places more emphasis on accuracy.

Variations

1. Centering the ball can be added to the punting drill.
2. Add competition by awarding a point for each kick traveling beyond a designated line during the exchange of kicks.
3. Add the return of kick.
   a. Designate one group as the kicking side, the other the kick-return side.
   b. The kicking side may punt or placekick; the kick-return side attempts to catch the kick on the fly.
   c. If the kicked ball hits the ground or is fumbled, the ball is recovered and sent back to the kicking side. (Note: In accordance with the rules, a kicked ball that is fumbled or hits the ground is dead and may not be played.)
   d. If the kicked ball is caught on the fly, the player making the catch runs in with the ball and exchanges places with the kicker.
   e. Continue until all punt, placekick, and receive.
   f. Variation: When the ball is caught on the fly, the kicker of that ball may attempt to down the ball carrier by pulling the flag as he/she runs in with the ball.

skill tests
6

By now you have probably been exposed not only to the many skills that comprise the game of REC Football but to the game itself. Obviously, the skills required of individual players in a flag or touch football game are somewhat peculiar to the position played. Nevertheless, how well you perform as a team member depends largely upon your ability to perform the individual skills of the game.

Now that you have been exposed to the proper technique of executing each skill and have practiced these in various drills, relays, and football related games, you will, no doubt, welcome the opportunity to evaluate your performance. Skill tests provide a means of determining your level of competence as well as your progress. Several of these, such as the variations of the tests that use a zone method of scoring and the centering and passing tests using targets, are designed as self-testing devices to help identify your strengths and weaknesses. These skill tests may also be used effectively for squad competition.

The pass receiving test and the zigzag run, like many of the others, may be used as warm-up drills. By doing so, you are given another opportunity to assess your consistency in skill performance.

The test items from the A.A.H.P.E.R. *Football Skills Test Manual* (*Starred) that lend themselves to flag and touch football determine your specific level of skill in these particular areas. However, in most instances, they require more time to administer.

FORWARD PASS FOR DISTANCE*

Purpose

To measure the distance a player can throw a forward pass.

Equipment

1. A properly marked playing field.
2. Footballs.

3. Measuring tape.
4. Marking stakes.

Testing Area

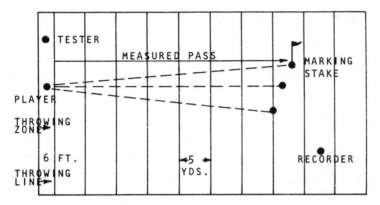

Test Description

1. A forward pass for distance is thrown from between two parallel lines 6 feet apart.
2. One or more running steps may be taken inside the zone prior to the throw.
3. The ball is thrown as far as possible without stepping over the line.
4. The player is allowed 3 passes.
5. The pass is marked at the point where the ball first hits the ground.
6. The longest pass is measured at right angles to the throwing line and recorded.

Scoring

The score is the distance in feet from the throwing line to the point where the longest pass hits the ground.

Variations

1. Take accuracy into consideration and determine the distance of the pass by subtracting the deviation from the intended line of flight perpendicular to the throwing line. (Note: This is easily done by stretching a rope from the intended line of flight to the spot of contact, then swinging an arc back to that line towards the thrower to determine the distance minus accuracy score.)
2. For expediency in determining the player's ability to throw a forward pass for distance, use the zone method of scoring.
   a. A playing field is marked with lines at three or more designated distances from the throwing line, as determined by the skill level of the players.
   b. Scoring method:
      (1) 3 points for landing beyond the third line
      (2) 2 points for landing between the second and third line

    (3) 1 point for landing between the first and second line
    (4) 0 points for landing between the throwing line and the first line
  c. The score is the total number of points gained from the three forward passes.

FOOTBALL PLACEKICK/PUNT FOR DISTANCE*

Purpose

To measure the distance a player can placekick/punt a football.

Equipment

1. A properly marked playing field.
2. Footballs.
3. A kicking tee.
4. Measuring tape.
5. Marking stakes.

Testing Area

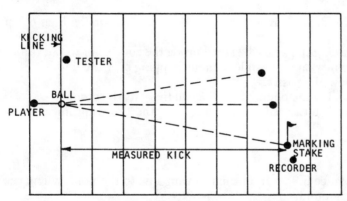

Test Description

Placekick
1. The ball is properly set up on a kicking tee on the kicking line midway of the field's sidelines.
2. The approach run taken prior to the kick may be as long as desired.

Punt
1. A punt for distance is made from within 6-foot kicking zone.
2. One or 2 steps may be taken inside the zone prior to the punt.

Placekick/Punt
3. The ball is kicked as far as possible.
4. The player is allowed 3 kicks.
5. The kick is marked at the point where the ball first hits the ground.
6. The longest kick is measured at right angles to the kicking line and recorded.

Scoring

The score is the distance in feet from the kicking line to the point where the longest kick hits the ground.

Variation

1. For expediency in determining the player's ability to kick a football for distance, use the zone method of scoring.
   a. A playing field is marked with lines at three or more designated distances from the kicking line, as determined by the skill level of the players.
   b. Scoring method:
      (1) 3 points for landing beyond the third line
      (2) 2 points for landing between the second and third line
      (3) 1 point for landing between the first and second line
      (4) 0 points for landing between the kicking line and the first line
   c. The score is the total number of points gained from the 3 kicks.
2. Take accuracy into consideration and determine the distance of the kick by subtracting the deviation from the intended line of flight perpendicular to the kicking line. (Note: This is easily done by stretching a rope from the intended line of flight to the spot of contact, then swinging an arc back to that line towards the punter to determine the distance minus accuracy score.)

PASS FOR ACCURACY

Purpose

1. To measure the player's ability to throw a forward pass at a target.
2. To measure the player's ability to execute a one-hand underhanded spiral lateral pass.

Equipment

1. An old tire or hoola hoop suspended from the ground with the bottom of the target about 4 feet from the ground.
2. Footballs.

Testing Area

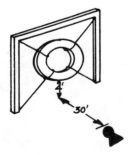

Test Description

1. The passer stands behind a line 30 feet from the target.
2. The player executes a pass at the target.
3. Five consecutive tries are allowed.
4. Balls passing through the target count 2 points while balls hitting the target but not going through count 1 point.
5. The maximum score is 10 points.
6. The distance of the throw may be increased as the skill increases.

Scoring

The score is the total number of points gained in executing 5 passes at the target.

CENTERING FOR ACCURACY

Purpose

To measure the player's ability to center a football at a target.

Equipment

1. An old tire or a hoola hoop suspended from the ground with the bottom of the target about 2 feet from the ground.
2. Footballs.

Testing Area

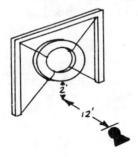

Test Description

1. The ball is placed on a line 12 feet in front of the target.
2. The player assumes a position over the ball and centers the ball at the target.
3. The player should abide by all rules governing the technique of centering.
4. Five consecutive tries are allowed.
5. Balls passing through the target count 2 points while balls hitting the target but not going through count 1 point.
6. The maximum score is 10 points.

Scoring

The score is the total number of points gained in centering the ball 5 times at the target.

PASS RECEIVING

Purpose

To measure a player's ability to receive a short pass.

Equipment

1. A smooth grass field properly marked as diagrammed.
2. Footballs.
3. Two cones to mark turning points.

Testing Area

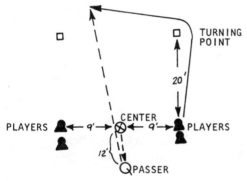

Test Description

NOTE: Success depends upon having one or more expert passers who can consistently pass to the same area of the field as the pass pattern is run.

1. The field is laid out as diagrammed with cones marking the two turning points, and throw-down bases or spots of lime marking the positions of the center, passer, and runners to the right and left of center.
2. The distance of the two turning points may be decreased or increased, as determined by the skill level of the players.
3. On the signal "hike," the center snaps the ball to the passer and the player runs straight ahead and around the turning point.
4. The pass receiver cuts around the near turning point and heads slightly to the outside of the other turning point and attempts to catch the pass.
5. The pass receiver alternates sides and is thrown 5 passes on each side.
6. The player need not try for poorly thrown balls.
7. Several players may be tested simultaneously to allow sufficient rest between tries.

Scoring

The score is the sum of passes caught from both sides.

ZIGZAG RUN

Purpose

To determine the player's ability to zigzag around obstacles while carrying a football.

Equipment

1. A smooth grass field properly marked as diagrammed.
2. Footballs.
3. Six cones.
4. Stopwatch.

Testing Area

5   10   15   20   25   30   YDS.

Test Description

1. Place 6 cones in a straight line 5 yards apart.
2. Player stands behind the starting line with the ball in his/her hands.
3. On the signal "go," the player runs around the obstacles in a zigzag fashion as shown in the diagram.
4. The ball may be carried in any way.
5. The player is allowed 10 seconds for the test.
6. One point is awarded for each obstacle passed during the 10 seconds.
7. Each player is allowed two tries.

Scoring

The score is the total number of points gained of the best of 2 tries while carrying a football around obstacles for 10 seconds.

After scoring yourself on the self-testing devices described in Chapter 6, how do you rate your skill in forward passing, place kicking, punting, and centering? What specific form of practice should you undertake to strengthen the weakest skills?

---

football related
games
7

You may be asking "Why football related games when it's the official game itself that I want to play?" Leaders who advocate the use of "lead-up" games to team sports do so for many reasons. In the case of REC Football, some of the reasons are:

1. The fundamental skills may be isolated to a certain degree and practiced in depth to attain greater perfection.
2. The playing area required is usually quite variable with regard to width and length and necessary markings.
3. The equipment used is minimal and if flag belts and flags are not available or not preferred, one-hand touch may be used.
4. The rules of the game are relatively simple.
5. The length of each game can vary according to the time available.
6. Officials are not required as in a regulation game.
7. Variations may be used according to player's interest.
8. The games are adaptable to many ages, skill levels, and coed groups.
9. The games are adaptable to small groups of 2-6 on a team and thus lend themselves to after-school and recreational use.
10. A greater number of players get to handle the ball more often than in an official REC Football game.
11. The players not included in the official game in progress may be involved in this type of game in an adjacent area.
12. The element of game strategy is developed gradually through football related games.
13. Last but not least, these games in themselves are both challenging and fun!

Many other football related games exist, but these have been carefully selected and adapted for REC Football. In most instances, the size of the playing area recommended for each game is readily available when the various lines and markings of the regulation REC Football field are utilized in part, running either its length or width.

CIRCLE CHASE

Skills

Flag pulling, running.

Equipment

Flag belts with flags.

Players

12 to 18.

Area

Area free of hazards and suitable for running.

Formation

Circle.

Rules

1. After forming a large circle, number off by threes.
2. When the leader calls a number, the players with that number run around the outside of the circle in a clockwise direction, trying to deflag as many runners ahead of them as possible before returning to their original position in the circle.
3. All runners return to and remain in their place in the circle while flags are replaced.
4. Only the runners not deflagged are eligible to run when their number is called again.
5. The leader keeps calling the different numbers until only one or two of each remains in the game.

Variation

1. Number off by fours or fives for a larger group and by twos for a smaller-size group.

FOOTBALL KEEP AWAY

Skills

Passing, receiving, covering a pass receiver, dodging, running, and flag pulling.

Equipment

Football, flag belts with flags of contrasting color to designate teams.

Players

Two teams of 3 to 6 players.

Area

Limited boundary lines, approximately 60 feet by 60 feet.

Formation

Scattered.

Rules

1. The object is for one team to keep the ball away from the opponents by dodging, running, and continuously passing and catching the football within the playing area.
2. The other team tries to intercept the ball or pull the flàg of the ball carrier.
3. The team intercepting a pass or pulling the ball carrier's flag gains possession of the ball.
4. The ball is declared dead when it touches the ground, and it goes over to the other team that was not in possession.
5. The ball is put back in play with a pass by a stationary and unguarded player.
6. During the game, the players verbally call out the consecutive completed passes.
7. The team making the greatest number of completed passes in succession wins.

Variation

1. Allow passing only, making it illegal to run with the ball or down the ball carrier. The player passing the ball is stationary and unguarded, but the receiver may be on the run until the ball is caught. To gain possession of the ball, the opponents must intercept a pass, since pulling the flag is no longer a means of stopping the ball carrier.

PUNT AND CATCH

Skills

Punting, receiving a punted ball (forward pass, receiving a forward pass).

Equipment

Footballs.

Players

Two teams of 6 to 8 players.

Area

Large rectangular playing area of variable lengths and widths, such as 90 feet by 150 feet or 105 feet by 210 feet with a 30-foot-wide neutral zone at midfield.

Formation

Each team is lined up in two lines covering the area between the neutral zone and its own goal.

Rules

1. The object is for players to punt the ball back and forth across the neutral zone into the other team's area.
2. The player closest to the ball attempts to catch it, and, if successful, punts it back over the neutral zone into the opponent's area.
3. If the punt receiver misses the punt and it touches the ground, the kicking side receives a point.
4. The ball is put back into play immediately by the player recovering the ball.
5. No score is made if the ball lands in thte neutral zone or outside the opponent's playing area.
6. A ball going out-of-bounds is put into play opposite the point it crossed the boundary line.
7. Points are made only by the kicking team when the ball lands on the ground in the opponent's area on the fly.
8. The players on each team may rotate in a clockwise direction each time the ball touches the ground in their area.
9. The team making the point calls aloud its own cumulative score.

Variations

1. Use a forward pass instead of the punt and call the game "Pass and Catch."
2. Use the punt and pass interchangeably in the same game.
3. Use two footballs simultaneously.

FIVE-STEP FOOTBALL

Skills

Punting, passing, and receiving a punted or passed ball.

Equipment

Football.

Players

Two teams of 2 to 8 players.

Area

A large rectangular playing area of variable lengths and widths, such as 30 yards by 50 yards or 35 yards by 60 yards; kicking lines marked at the points halfway between the goal line and the center of the field.

Formation

Players are scattered in their own area of the field to protect their goal line, but move up and down the entire length of the field in order to be in the best position to play the ball.

Rules

1. The object is for the players of one team to pass or punt the ball over the opposing team's goal line without the ball being caught.
2. To begin the game, and after each point is scored, the ball is put into play by a pass or punt from the kicking line.
3. The receiving team may be no closer than 30 feet from the player who is passing or punting the ball.
4. If a player succeeds in catching the ball on the fly, he/she is allowed to take 5 giant steps toward the opponent's goal line before passing or punting the ball.
5. If the ball hits the ground before being touched or if a ball is fumbled while being caught, the first player who touched it must pass or punt from the point where it was first touched.
6. If the ball bounds across the goal line, it is put into play on the goal line.
7. If a passed or kicked ball crosses the goal line on the fly and is caught behind the goal line, the player who caught it takes the 5 steps from the goal line.
8. Play continues with the ball being passed or punted back and forth from one team to the other until a point is scored.
9. A pass or punt that touches the ground behind the opponent's goal line on the fly scores 1 point.
10. After a goal is scored, the team scored against is given a choice of kicking off or receiving.
11. The winner is the team with the greatest number of points at the end of the playing period.

Variations

1. Limit the method of playing the ball to passing only.
2. Limit the method of playing the ball to punting only.

TWENTY-YARD FOOTBALL

Skills

Centering, passing, receiving, handing off, lateraling, ball carrying, and flag pulling.

Equipment

Football, flag belts with flags of contrasting color to designate teams.

Players

Two teams of 3 to 5 players.

Area

A rectangular playing area 20 yards long by 25 yards wide.

Formation

Each team in scrimmage formation.

Rules

1. The object is for one team to cross the goal line 20 yards away in 4 downs or less.
2. The ball is put into play by a scrimmage from the goal line of the team that puts the ball into play.
3. In general, the rules are the same as for REC Football.
4. The team has 4 tries to make a goal by running with the ball, handing off, lateraling, or by passing from behind the line of scrimmage.
5. When the offensive team fails to score in 4 downs or when the defending team intercepts a pass, the defending team puts the ball into scrimmage from its own goal line.
6. When a goal is scored, the team scored against puts the ball into play by a scrimmage from its own goal line.
7. Each goal counts 6 points.

FORWARD PASS FOOTBALL

Skills

Centering, forward pass, receiving, and covering a pass receiver.

Equipment

Football, colored scrimmage vests or pinnies to designate teams.

Players

Two teams of 3 to 7 players.

Area

Rectangular playing area approximately 40 yards wide by 50 yards long with a midfield line.

Formation

Each team in scrimmage formation at the midfield line.

Rules

1. The object is to move the ball by completing forward passes and to score by completing a pass behind the opponent's goal line.
2. One team starts the game at midfield by centering the ball to the passer.
3. The passer is not allowed to run and the defensive team is not allowed to rush the passer, but the ball must be passed within a slow count of five (one-thousand-one, one-thousand-two, etc.), or the opposing team is awarded the ball.
4. The pass receiver may not run with the ball after it is caught.
5. All completed forward passes give the offensive team another down with the ball put in play at the point the pass was completed.
6. The opposing team takes possession of the ball on an incomplete or inter-cepted pass at the place of the last play.
7. A touchdown is scored when one team completes a pass beyond the oppo-nent's goal line.
8. After each touchdown the opponent's of the scoring team start play again at midfield by centering the ball.

flickerball
8

Flickerball is played with a football and incorporates many features of basketball, football, speedball, and hockey. The object is to advance the ball by passing to a position from which a goal shot may be attempted. The team scoring the most points wins. Any player on either team is allowed to handle the ball at any time. The ball may be advanced toward the goal only by passing. The player in control of the ball is not allowed to advance toward the goal while in possession of the ball. However, the ball may be carried laterally or backward. No contact is allowed and, with refinement, the game is an extremely fluid sport in which lightning passes, sudden starts and stops, and rather close man-to-man play predominate. All players have countless opportunities to pass and receive the football.

One of the novel features of Flickerball is that an attempted goal results in loss of possession of the ball, since the goals are situated out-of-bounds. Any shot, successful or unsuccessful, result in loss of the ball for the shooting team. Thus, the offensive team is forced to eliminate wild or haphazard shooting and work for better scoring opportunities. After a goal attempt, the defensive team puts the ball in play by throwing inbounds from behind its own end line.

Another interesting feature is that a loose ball that remains on the playing field is a free ball and may be played by any player. This provision promotes fluidity of action and places a premium on quick reaction and alertness. Running and physical stamina is an important consideratiton in any team's success in Flickerball.

FLICKERBALL RULES

The object is to advance the ball by forward passes to a position from which a goal may be scored.

Rule 1: Field, Players, and Equipment

Section 1 The field shall be a rectangular area with lines and goals, as shown in figure 8.1.

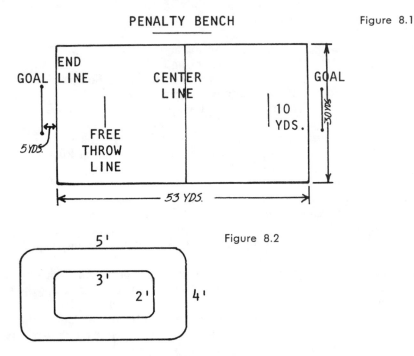

Figure 8.1

PENALTY BENCH

Figure 8.2

Section 2   Goals may be made of any durable material, such as 3/4-inch plywood, plastic, fiberglass, or metal and painted a bright color. Dimensions are shown in figure 8.2. The goals are supported on pipe so that the lower part of the opening is 8 feet above the ground. All corners are rounded with a 6-inch radius.

Section 3   The official ball is a regulation leather or rubber football.

Section 4   Regular athletic clothing and tennis shoes are worn. No hard shoes are permitted.

Section 5   The game shall be played by two teams of 7 players each: right, center, and left forwards; the center; and right, center, and left guards.

Rule 2:   Definitions

Section 1: Backcourt   The defensive area from the center line to the end line from where a team defends its goal.

Section 2: Ball Picked Up   A player starts the game from a dead ball situation. The ball is dead until lifted off the ground.

Section 3: Delaying the Game   Whereby a team stops play from continuing in order to gain an unfair advantage.

Section 4: Diving on the Ball   An illegal act of moving your body in an effort to retrieve the ball.

Section 5: Freezing the Ball   Whereby a team maintains possession of the ball without attempting to score.

Section 6: Front Court   The offensive area from the center line to the end line toward the offensive team's goal.

Section 7: Fumble   The act of dropping the ball after possession has clearly been made.

Section 8: Game Goal   A score made during active play.

Section 9: Goal Attempt   The act of shooting for a score.

Section 10: Goaltending   The act of a defensive player positioning himself out-of-bounds in an effort to block an attempted goal.

Section 11: Held Ball   Whereby two or more players hold the ball in such a manner that play is stopped.

Section 12: Intentionally Grounding the Ball   Whereby a player deliberately grounds the ball to renew his parallel five-second possession or his team's ten-second backcourt position of the ball.

Section 13: Intentionally Kicking the Ball   Whereby a player intentionally propels the ball with his foot in an effort to gain possession of it.

Section 14: Intentionally Pushing the Ball   Whereby a player intentionally pushes the ball with his hands in an effort to gain possession of it.

Section 15: Muff   The act of dropping the ball when attempting to catch it, and possession of the ball is never made.

Section 16: Out-of-bounds Rule   Rule for putting a dead ball back into play. Although called "out-of-bounds," this rule applies equally to putting the ball in play from out-of-bounds or from any position on the field of play.

Section 17: Overhand Shot   The act of a player throwing the ball at the goal with one hand. Any football type pass above the shoulder line is considered overhand. Push shots and hook shots, etc. are not legal shots.

Section 18: Penalty Goal   A score made during an inactive part of the game as a result of a foul.

Section 19: Personal Contact   The act of one-player contacting another.

Section 20: Traveling   The act of taking more than the allowable amount of steps toward your goal while you have the ball in your possession.

Rule 3: Scoring

Section 1   A goal is scored when a player passes the ball from within the playing area and it goes into or hits the face of the board. A ball that enters the hole in the board counts 3 points. A goal that hits the face of the board but does not enter the hole is worth 1 point. An overhand shot must be used (fig. 8.3).

Section 2   A 3-point goal is awarded to the shooting team when a defensive player goal tends.

Section 3   A goal attempt that is blocked by a defensive player and remains on the field of play is a free ball and may be played by any player.

Section 4   A goal attempt that is blocked by a defensive player and goes out-of-bounds is given to the defensive team out-of-bounds at the point where the ball went out.

Section 5   A penalty goal is scored the same as a field goal. The penalty goal is attempted from a line parallel to the end line and 10 yards distance, in front of goal (15 yards from the goal). After a penalty throw, possession of the ball is given to the offended team out-of-bounds at the nearest free throw line except for a flagrant foul or unsportsmanlike conduct.

Figure 8.3

Rule 4: Timing of the Game

Section 1   The game shall consist of two 20-minute halves. Time is out whenever the ball is not in play.

Section 2   Each team is allowed two 2-minute time-outs per half. Each extra time-out is a technical foul. Team captains cannot call time-out during active play unless a player is injured. In the event of an injury, the time-out is charged to the referee.

Section 3   The clock is stopped only for team time-outs, all personal and technical fouls, an injury, an official time-out, and in cases where the ball leaves the playing field by a great distance.

Section 4   In case of a tie at the end of regulation play, the game shall go into overtime. A period of 3 minutes is played after a 5-minute rest. In case of a tie at the end of two overtime periods, a "sudden death" period is played; the first team to score wins the game.

Rule 5: Substitutions

Section 1   Substitutitons may be made any time the ball is dead.

Section 2   Any number of players may be substituted at one time.

Section 3   Substitutes shall enter the game within 5 yards of the center line only. Players may leave the game from any area.

Section 4   After a substitution of several players, a team captain may ask for a team line-up. This action is granted provided the opposing captain approves.

Can you pick out elements in Flickerball that are derived from each of these sports: basketball, football, speedball, and hockey?

Section 5   A player in the penalty box may not be substituted for until he reenters the game. If a player is ejected from the game, his substitute takes his place in the penalty box.

Sction 6   Players in the penalty box may reenter the game after a game goal is scored by either team, or at half-time. In case of an overtime game, players may reenter the game at the end of the last half.

Section 7   It is the responsibility of the players to complete a substitution before the ball becomes active again.

Rule 6:   Putting Ball In Play

Section 1   A jump ball is used to start the game, the second half, and in all held ball situations (fig. 8.4).

Section 2   The ball (ends pointing toward goals) is tossed up between two players. The first player obtaining the ball must pass the ball laterally, as it cannot be thrown forward nor carried into the backcourt. A player other than a jumper must touch the ball after the jump before either jumper may again handle the ball. In the event that both players miss the ball at the toss-up, a rejump is called.

Section 3   Players other than the jumpers must remain outside of an imaginary 10-foot diameter circle until the ball is batted.

Section 4   No one is permitted to advance toward his goal while ball is in his control. The player with the ball may move only in a lateral or backward direction. A player who gains control of the ball while advancing toward his goal is allowed a maximum of one and one-half steps in which to stop his advance or to swerve to a lateral direction.

Figure 8.4

Section 5   If a player is called for traveling, the offending player must place the ball on the ground in order that opponents can immediately put the ball in play.

Section 6   No player is allowed to possess the ball more than 5 seconds at any one time during active play when closely guarded.

Section 7   A ball whistled dead on the field of play or out-of-bounds remains dead until picked up by a player entitled to put it in play. After the official grounds the ball, the player putting the ball in play has 5 seconds to lift the ball off the ground and 5 seconds more to throw the ball. All players must be 3 feet away from the man putting the ball in play until he picks the ball up. Player putting the ball in play cannot move from this position until he throws the ball. He can, however, pivot on either foot in any direction.

Section 8   "Out-of-bounds" rules apply when ball is put in play anywhere on the field or out-of-bounds after certain dead ball situations.

A. When the ball is out-of-bounds or dead in the frontcourt, a player putting the ball in play must throw the ball laterally or backwards.
B. When the ball is out-of-bounds or dead in the backcourt, a player may throw anywhere, forward or laterally, as long as the receiver is in the backcourt. If a pass goes into the frontcourt on the initial throw, it is returned to the spot where the pass started and given to the other team.

Section 9   A team putting ball in play in backcourt is given 10 seconds to advance the ball into its front court. This 10-second timing does not begin until ball has been thrown into play. Penalty for failure to advance the ball within 10 seconds is loss of ball at spot of infraction.

Section 10   After the ball has advanced past the center line into the frontcourt, the offensive team must continue to play ball in this area until a shot at the goal is attempted or until the ball is lost to defense. The penalty for the offensive team passing or carrying the ball back into the backcourt after the ball has been advanced into the frontcourt is loss of ball at a point on the center line where the ball passed into the backcourt.

Section 11   When a team is given possession of the ball out-of-bounds, it is given 5 seconds to put the ball into play. Penalty is loss of ball at the spot the ball went out-of-bounds.

Rule 7: Passes

Section 1   If the offensive team attempts a forward pass that is incomplete (without interference on the part of a defensive player), possession of the ball is given immediately to a player of the defensive team. The ball is not dead until it touches the ground and is put into play at the spot where it touched the ground.

Section 2   If a forward pass is incomplete because a defensive player is the cause of the incompletion, the ball remains a free ball. It can be played by either team, unless it rolls out-of-bounds, in which case the "out-of-bounds" rule applies.

Section 3   An incomplete lateral pass that remains on the field of play is a free ball and may be played by any player.

Section 4   Any fumbled ball that remains on the field of play is a free ball and may be played by any player.

Section 5   In cases where receiver of pass is bound by the rules to receive it within a certain area, he must gain definite control of ball within that area.

Section 6   When ball goes out-of-bounds, the opponent of the player who last touched ball inbounds will be given possession at that out-of-bounds point.

Rule 8:   Dead Ball Situations

Section 1   The following are situations in which the ball is whistled dead:

A.   Traveling
B.   Personal foul
C.   Technical foul
D.   Out-of-bounds ball
E.   Incomplete forward pass (with no interference on part of defensive player)
F.   Signaling of time-out or end of playing time
G.   Violation of "out-of-bounds" rules
H.   Violation of "five-seconds" rule (individual possession)
I.   Violation of "backcourt" rule (10-second rule)
J.   Held ball
K.   If an official inadvertently or mistakenly blows the whistle, play is stopped. The ball is put in play by the team that had possession, or if it was a free ball, a jump ball situation is called.

Rule 9:   Fouls

Section 1   Personal fouls are personal contact, "kicking" or pushing the ball, and diving on a loose ball. Four personal fouls disqualify a player from any further participation in the game, including overtime.

Section 2   Personal contact occurs when any player causes physical contact with an opponent.

A.   Defensive—Overguarding or charging any offensive player with or without the ball.
B.   Offensive—Charging or butting any defensive player.
C.   Intentional body contact with one's own team members is a personal foul when the action is made to stretch existing rules.

Section 3   If an offensive player is contacted in the act of shooting a goal, a personal foul is charged to the offending player. The goal, if good, shall count and the shooting player is given one free shot at the goal. After the penalty shot, the defensive team takes possession of the ball on its own end line.

Section 4   If an offensive player contacts a defensive player while in the act of shooting, the goal does not count. The defensive team takes control of the ball at the point of infraction.

Section 5   Diving on a loose ball constitutes a foul. The team not guilty of the infraction takes possession of the ball at that point.

Section 6   Any player committing a personal foul must leave the game and cannot return to the field of play until a field goal is made by either team. A penalty goal does not allow a player to return to the game. The player remains in the penalty box until he returns to play. He cannot be substituted for while in the penalty box. Players in the penalty box at halftime may return to the game at the start of the second half.

Section 7   Double personal fouls cancel each other.

Section 8   For a personal foul by either defensive or offensive players, the offended team receives possession of the ball. Play begins at point of infraction and the ball is put in play as soon as the offending player leaves the playing field.

Section 9   Reasons for technical fouls are:

A. Too many men on field.
B. Too many time-outs.
C. Delay of the game.
D. Illegal substitution.
E. Intentional grounding of the ball.
F. Player, other than team captain, talking to officials.
G. A player standing less than 3 feet away from a dead ball or the man putting the ball in play after the first warning (delay of game).
H. A player standing less than 10 feet away from jump ball when it is put in play after the first warning (delay of game).
I. Diving on a loose ball.
J. Intentional kicking the ball.
K. Flagrant foul.
L. Unsportsmanlike conduct.

Section 10   One penalty shot is given to the offended team for a technical foul. Any player may shoot. The thrower remains behind the free throw line until the ball is dead (crossing the end line). The score does not count if the thrower steps on or over the free throw line. All other players remain behind the free throw line. If the thrower's teammate is ahead of the line, the penalty goal does not count. If an opponent is ahead of the free-throw line, the thrower has the option of taking his first score or shooting again. The ball is given to offending team at their end line (Exception: Rule 9, Section 12).

Section 11   Double technical fouls cancel each other and the ball is put in play by a center jump on the center line.

Can you name 4 situations in flickerball in which the ball is whistled dead? Can you name 7 situations? 11?

Section 12   Any fouls, personal or technical, by any player that is construed by an official to be flagrant or an act of unsportsmanlike conduct is handled as follows. The player is ejected from the game. His substitute goes to the penalty box until a field goal is scored. A free throw is given to the offended team. After the free throw, successful or not, the offended team takes possession of the ball out-of-bounds at a point opposite its free throw line.

Rule 10: Coed Flickerball Rules

Coed Flickerball is played with the following exceptions.

Section 1 A team shall consist of 7 players: 4 males and 3 females.

Section 2 Females must play the ball at least once in a scoring possession.

Section 3 Males cannot score from inside the 30-foot penalty area.

Rule 11: Indoor Flickerball

Indoor Flickerball is played with the following exceptions.

Section 1 Indoor Flickerball is played on a regulation basketball court with 2 teams of 5 players each. (The indoor coed game is played with 3 females and 3 males).

Section 2 The goal is mounted on the basketball backboard with the bottom of the hole 8 feet from the floor.

Section 3 A line is drawn parallel to and 15 feet from each end line. Play may take place in this area, but all goals attempted must emanate from outside this area.

Rule 12: Officiating

Section 1 There shall be a minimum of 3 officials for Flickerball games: the head referee, a second referee, and the scorekeeper.

Section 2 The head referee shall be responsible for the overall conduct of the game and may amend or change other officials' calls as he sees it. The head referee checks the field and goals for safety, checks players for safe equipment, briefs team captains, flips coin for choice of goals, officiates the game, and is responsible to cancel the game in case of inclement weather when the game is in progress.

Section 3 The second referee is responsible to assist the head referee in pregame functions; assist in officiating the game; time the game; keep count of 5- and 10-second possession violations; and notify the game scorer of score, time-outs, and personal fouls.

Section 4 The official scorekeeper will keep track of score, time-outs, and personal fouls. It is the scorekeeper's responsibility to notify the head referee when a team has exceeded its time-outs and when a player has four personal fouls.

glossary

The REC Football player will want to acquire a thorough understanding of the following terms. Although many of the terms are common to tackle football, some are unique to flag and touch football.

Backfield line. An imaginary line one yard behind and parallel to the scrimmage line of the offensive team.

Backfield player. A player at least one yard from the line of scrimmage.

Batting. The act of striking the ball with a hand or arm.

Blocking. The act of preventing, by body position, an opponent from touching or pulling the flag of the ball carrier.

Center. The player who puts the ball in play at the line of scrimmage with a ball snap.

Centering. The act of putting the ball in play other than by a kick-off.

Clipping. The illegal act of running or diving into the back, or throwing or dropping the body across the back of the leg or legs of an opponent.

Conversion. A running or passing play attempted from the 10-yard line after a touchdown is scored. A ball moved beyond the goal line before becoming dead counts 2 points; moved beyond the 5-yard line counts 1 point.

Dead ball. When play is stopped because of situations such as the ball touching the ground, an incompleted pass, a fumbled reception of a kick, a flag being pulled, etc.

Defensive team. The team without possession of the ball.

Down. A unit of play that begins with the centering of the ball and ends when the ball is dead.

Ends. The players on the line of scrimmage who are closer to each sideline than the other players.

Fair catch. The act of a player on the receiving team extending one arm and a hand clearly above the head to signal his/her intention to catch but not advance the kick.

Flags. The equipment worn by each player on a belt. Each member of a team wears the same color, but the flags for the two teams are of contrasting color.

Flag guarding. An illegal act whereby the ball carrier uses hands, arms, clothing or spinning to prevent an opponent from pulling the flag.

Flag pulling. The act of stopping the ball carrier by detaching one of the flags while at least one foot of the player pulling the flag is in contact with the ground.

Flanker back. The name of the offensive backfield player who lines up laterally to the quarterback and outside the end.

Flat pass. A ball with little trajectory thrown in the area outside the ends and no farther than 10 yards down field.

Floater. A thrown ball with high trajectory and decreased force.

Forward pass. A pass from any player behind the line of scrimmage toward the opponent's goal.

Foul. Any infringement of the rules that results in the loss of yardage or the loss of a down.

Free ball. A live ball, other than a forward pass, not in a player's possession.

Free kick. A kick made under restrictions that prohibit either team from advancing beyond established restraining lines until the ball is kicked. A free kick may be either a punt or a placekick.

Fullback. The name of the offensive backfield player who is usually lined up directly behind the quarterback.

Fumble. Losing control of the ball while running or while receiving a center, lateral pass, kick, or handoff.

Guard. The offensive lineman on either side of the center who usually blocks for the backs.

Halfback. The name of the offensive backfield player whose alignment is either to the right or left of center.

Handoff. The act of handing the ball to a teammate whereby both players momentarily have their hands on the ball. Behind the line of scrimmage the ball may be handed forward to a backfield player, but beyond the line of scrimmage the teammate receiving the handoff must be either parallel to or behind the ball carrier.

Hike. The signal given to the center from the quarterback to begin the act of centering; also the act of centering.

Huddle. The means by which two or more players confer between downs to designate the next play.

Hurdling. An attempt by the runner to jump with both feet or knees foremost over a player who is still on his/her feet.

Illegal motion. The movement by any member of the offensive team, other than one backfield player, one second immediately before the ball is centered.

Lateral pass. A pass thrown sideways or back toward the passer's own goal.

Linebacker. The name of the defensive player who lines up between the linemen and the safety and attempts to stop the ball carrier or break up passes.

Line player. A player whose position is at the line of scrimmage at the beginning of each play.

Line of scrimmage. An imaginary line that passes through the front tip of the ball and is parallel to the goal line.

Man-to-man. A defensive team technique that involves a player covering (guarding) an individual opponent.

Muff. An unsuccessful attempt to catch or recover a ball, which is touched in the attempt; ball is dead at the spot.

Offensive team. The team in possession of the ball.

Offside. A foul committed anytime a member of either team enters the neutral zone and does not return before the ball is centered.

Option. The offended team's choice of taking the play or the penalty resulting from a foul.

Own goal. The goal a team is defending.

Pass interference. The act in which a player pushes, blocks illegally, removes a flag, or holds an opponent to prevent him/her from catching or intercepting a pass.

Interference may occur anytime from the time the ball leaves the hand of the passer until it is touched by another player.

Penalty enforcement reference spots:

    a. *Dead ball spot:* The point at which the ball last became dead

    b. *Enforcement spot:* The point from which the penalty for a foul is enforced

    c. *Previous spot:* The point from which the ball was last put in play

    d. *Spot of the foul:* The point at which the foul occurred

    e. *Succeeding spot:* The point at which the ball would next be put in play if that foul had not occurred.

Personal contact. Any contact between opponents including the use of hands and arms to prevent movement by holding and pushing.

Pitch out. A lateral pass that is used in a particular play.

Placekick. The act of putting the ball in play by a kick whereby the ball is held for the kicker by a teammate or by a kicking tee.

Punt. The act of putting the ball in play by a kick whereby the ball is dropped toward the ground and contacted before it touches the ground.

Quarterback. The name of the player who calls signals to execute a play.

Receiver. A person who catches or attempts to catch a pass or a kick.

Rusher. The name of the defensive line player who moves quickly to touch or to pull the flag of the ball carrier.

Safety. Counts two points and occurs when a ball legally in possession of a player becomes dead behind his/her own goal line, provided the impetus which sent it across was given by a member of his/her own team; also the position of a player on the defensive team who lines up behind the linebacker.

Screening. The act of protecting the ball carrier by body position alone, since use of the arms is illegal.

Scrimmage. The act of putting the ball in play.

Scrimmage kick. An announced kick, either a punt or a placekick, made by a team during a scrimmage down before team possession changes.

Shift. A simultaneous change of position by two or more offensive players after the ball is ready for play and before the snap.

Signal. The term used by the quarterback to indicate a play; also the sign to the center to start play.

Snapping the ball. The act of handing or passing the ball back from its position on the ground with a quick and continuous motion of the hand or hands. The ball must pass between the center's legs, may not be raised to more than a 45-degree angle at the snap, and the long axis of the ball must be at right angles to the scrimmage line.

Spiral pass. A type of pass or center that spins about the long axis in flight.

Stance. The position that both offensive and defensive players, other than the offensive center, must be in prior to the ball snap. The players must be on their feet with neither hand touching the ground at the snap. It is permissable for a player's hands to be on his/her knees.

Time-out. The period of time when the ball is dead and the game clock is stopped.

Touchback. A punt that is fumbled or lands in the end zone provided the impetus which sent it across the goal line was given by the opponents.

Touchdown. Counts 6 points and occurs when a runner carries the ball across the goal line or when a pass is completed in the end zone.

Touching. The act of stopping the ball carrier by placing one or both hands anywhere while at least one foot of the toucher is in contact with the ground.

Tripping. The act of using the lower leg or foot to obstruct an opponent below the knees.

Zone. A defensive team technique that involves a player covering (guarding) an area of the field; also the four marked areas on the field 20 yards in width.

questions
and answers

REC Football Examination

TRUE-FALSE

If the statement is completely true, encircle the "T" in the left hand margin. If the statement is false or partially false, encircle the "F." Each correct answer counts one point.

T   F   1. REC Football was developed so that coaches could legally have their players practice during the off-season. (p. 1)

T   F   2. The playing time for REC Football is 60 minutes plus time for intermission at the half. (p. 24)

T   F   3. Touching or pulling the flag is substituted for tackling in REC Football. (p. 25)

T   F   4. Each period in REC Football starts with a kick-off. (p. 24)

T   F   5. In an offensive stance the lineman's feet should be staggered as in a track start. (p. 15)

T   F   6. A forward pass may not be thrown if the ball is first run across the line of scrimmage. (p. 28)

T   F   7. Traveling is called if a ball carrier attempts to advance the ball after he/she has been downed. (p. 29)

T   F   8. The offensive team cannot be called for pass interference. (p. 28)

T   F   9. A player who runs out-of-bounds loses 5 yards as a penalty. (p. 25)

T   F 10. A player is not allowed to cross the line of scrimmage before the snap. (p. 27)

T   F 11. When a pass is in the air anyone is eligible to catch it. (p. 28)

T   F 12. A fumbled ball that goes out-of-bounds belongs to the last player who touched it. (p. 25)

T F 13. The quarterback must receive the snap on each offensive play. (p. 27)

T F 14. A handoff made behind the line of scrimmage may be executed in any direction. (p. 27)

T F 15. In executing a punt, the ball should be contacted diagonally across the instep of the punter's foot. (p. 13)

T F 16. The quarterback is the only player who can throw a pass. (p. 27)

T F 17. A lateral is only legal behind the line of scrimmage. (p. 28)

T F 18. The referee assumes a position behind the offensive team during play and watches the play near the ball. (p. 35)

T F 19. A team has 30 seconds to get the ball into play after it has been declared ready for play by the referee. (p. 25)

T F 20. The umpire should be responsible for keeping accurate count of downs and making sure that the down markers are accurate. (p. 36)

T F 21. A team cannot score if it is on defense. (p. 23)

T F 22. The head linesman takes a position behind the defensive team in REC Football. (p. 37)

T F 23. A ball carrier who steps on the sideline is out-of-bounds. (p. 25)

T F 24. An offensive player may use his/her hands when blocking in REC Football. (p. 31)

T F 25. The referee administers all penalties and explains options to captains when entitled following a foul. (p. 35)

T F 26. A free kick may be either a punt or a placekick. (p. 26)

T F 27. A successful conversion by passing counts more points than by running. (p. 23)

T F 28. In REC Football all players are eligible pass receivers. (p. 28)

T F 29. When playing the touch version of REC Football, the ball carrier must be tagged with both hands above the waist. (p. 25)

T F 30. The winner of a tie game is the team having the most earned first downs. (p. 24)

MULTIPLE-CHOICE

Choose the answer that best completes the sentence (1-17) or that best answers the question (18-25). Place the letter of that response in the corresponding blank. Each correct answer counts 2 points.

_____ 1. REC Football originated in
   a. Great Britain
   b. the United States
   c. Russia
   d. Poland   (p. 1)

_____ 2. REC Football is an outgrowth of
  a. basketball
  b. volleyball
  c. speedball
  d. regulation football (p. 1)

_____ 3. A touchdown is worth
  a. 1 point
  b. 2 points
  c. 6 points
  d. 7 points (p. 23)

_____ 4. A touchback is worth
  a. 0 points
  b. 1 point
  c. 2 points
  d. 6 points (p. 23)

_____ 5. The restraining line for the kicking team is the
  a. goal line
  b. quarter line
  c. center line
  d. 10 yard line (p. 26)

_____ 6. In order to earn another set of downs, the offensive team must make the next zone in
  a. 3 downs
  b. 4 downs
  c. 5 downs
  d. 6 downs (p. 26)

_____ 7. A player should signal a fair catch with
  a. both hands
  b. one hand raised above the head
  c. one foot
  d. a verbal announcement

_____ 8. Forward passes may be thrown from
  a. any point on the field
  b. at least 1 yard behind the line of scrimmage
  c. 5 yards behind the scrimmage line
  d. anywhere behind the scrimmage line (p. 27)

_____ 9. If the football is kicked over the goal line, it is placed on the
  a. 15-yard line
  b. 20-yard line
  c. 25-yard line
  d. 35-yard line (p. 26)

_____10. In a man-to-man defense, the player responsible for the quarterback is
  a. the middle linebacker
  b. one of the rushers
  c. one of the safeties
  d. one of the cornerbacks (p. 49)

_____11. The official most likely to call infractions on downfield plays is the
  a. referee
  b. umpire
  c. timer
  d. linesman (p. 37)

_____12. If a punt receiver catches the ball on his/her own 5-yard line and, in attempting to elude the defensive end, runs behind his/her own goal line and is touched there, it is ruled a
a. field goal
b. safety
c. touchdown
d. touchback

_____13. A flanker is an offensive back playing
a. behind the quarterback
b. between one guard and an end
c. outside of an end
d. between the center and a guard (p. 3)

_____14. The ball is put in play at the start of the game at the
a. goal line
b. conversion line
c. quarter line
d. center line (p. 24)

_____15. While waiting in position for the snap, the offensive lineman should
a. look at the ball
b. look at the man he/she is to screen
c. look at an object downfield
d. close the eyes and listen (p. 5)

_____16. When a violation of the rules takes place, the captain of the offended team may
a. take the penalty
b. take the play
c. take the play or the penalty
d. not have a choice as the referee tells what to do (p. 33)

_____17. In considering which play to call, the quarterback should *not* consider the
a. down
b. opponent's defense
c. crowd noise
d. yardage (p. 47)

_____18. Team B is kicking. One of the players of Team B crosses the restraining line before the ball is kicked. What is the penalty?
a. The kick is repeated from 5 yards behind the line.
b. The receiving team can take the play.
c. A first down is awarded where the ball was declared dead.
d. The captain has the option of either A or C.

_____19. The defensive team is charged with pass interference. What penalty does the referee administer?
a. The offensive team receives the ball at the spot of the foul and a first down
b. The offensive team receives the ball 15 yards from the line of scrimmage.
c. The offensive team gets the ball 15 yards from the spot of the foul.
d. The captain of the offensive team has the option of either A or B. (p. 28)

_____20. A player dives for the ball. What is the penalty?
   a. There is no penalty, but the team is warned that on the next offense there will be a 15-yard loss.
   b. There is a loss of 5 yards from the line of scrimmage.
   c. There is a loss of 10 yards from the line of scrimmage.
   d. There is a loss of 15 yards from the spot of the foul.   (p. 30)

_____21. A ball carrier runs over a set defensive player. What is the penalty, if any?
   a. The offensive team loses 15 yards because the team in possession of the ball is responsible for any contact made.
   b. Each team loses 10 yards.
   c. The fouls cancel each other and the down is replayed.
   d. The fouls cancel each other and the down advances.   (p. 30)

_____22. A player throws a forward pass after crossing the line of scrimmage. It is intercepted. What is the correct procedure for the referee to follow?
   a. The interception is nullified because the pass was illegal. The offensive team is penalized.
   b. The intercepting team gets the ball.
   c. The captain of the intercepting team has the option of retaining possession of the ball or accepting the penalty.
   d. The intercepting team is given possession of the ball at the spot where the infraction occurred.

_____23. One of the members of the passing team interferes with an opponent intercepting a pass. What procedure should the referee use?
   a. The passing team loses the ball at the spot where the infraction occurred.
   b. The passing team is penalized 15 yards from the spot of the infraction or line of scrimmage, whichever is greater. Loss of down.
   c. The passing team is penalized 10 yards, from the spot of infraction or line of scrimmage, whichever is greater. Loss of down.
   d. The passing team is penalized 15 yards from the spot of infraction or line of scrimmage, whichever is greater. Down remains the same.
                                                              (p. 28)

_____24. A team punts the ball but does not announce its intention to punt to the referee. What is the penalty?
   a. There is a loss of 5 yards from the spot where the infraction occurred. The kick is repeated from that spot.
   b. There is a loss of the ball at the line of scrimmage.
   c. There is a loss of the ball 5 yards beyond the original line of scrimmage.
   d. There is a loss of the ball and a 10-yard penalty from the spot where the ball was declared dead.   (p. 27)

_____25. What is the penalty if a member of the defensive team crosses the line of scrimmage before the ball is snapped?
   a. There is an immediate loss of 5 yards and the down advances.
   b. There is an immediate loss of 5 yards and the down remains the same.
   c. There is an immediate loss of 10 yards and the down remains the same.
   d. The down advances but there is no loss of yardage.

MATCHING

Match the proper term in the right-hand column with the definition in the left-hand column. Place the identifying letter in the blank provided. Each correct answer counts 2 points.

_____ 1. Imaginary line that extends across the field at the point of the ball.   (p. 93)

_____ 2. Offensive back who lines up outside the end.   (p. 92)

_____ 3. An offensive maneuver in which a pass receiver pivots back toward the line of scrimmage.   (p. 43)

_____ 4. Team with the ball.   (p. 42)

_____ 5. A violation in which the offensive or defensive player moves forward before the ball is snapped.   (p. 27)

_____ 6. Player on the offensive team who ordinarily receives the ball snap.   (p. 93)

_____ 7. An offensive maneuver to protect the ball carrier.   (p. 93)

_____ 8. Defensive player responsible for covering the end when playing man-to-man. (p. 49)

_____ 9. The offensive lineman on either side of the center who usually blocks for the backs.   (p. 42)

_____ 10. The distance from one goal line to the other goal line.   (p. 22)

A. Fullback

B. 80 yards

C. Guard

D. Defense

E. Flanker

F. Screen

G. 100 yards

H. Quarterback

I. Submarine

J. Scrimmage line

K. Offense

L. Cornerback

M. Starting line

N. Button hook

O. Illegal motion

ANSWERS TO EVALUATION QUESTIONS
Answer and Page Reference

Page

5   The offensive stance for an Interior Linesman is with the feet shoulder width apart; for an End or a Back the feet are spread about 12 inches apart; for a Center, the feet are very far apart.   (pp. 4-5)

8   The Center is least ready to move quickly because the center of gravity is low and the base is wide, both of which make for stability.   (p. 5)

9   No Answer.

10   Some principles that apply to all passes are: focus your eyes on the target; step toward the target as you throw; aim to the side away from the defender; fake to disguise your intentions; aim ahead of the direction in which the receiver is moving.   (pp. 7-8)

16   Aim high with the wind and low into the wind when punting. Position yourself close to the line of scrimmage for the kick.   (p. 14)

33   See these pages for illustrations of hand signals.   (pp. 38-39)

35   The play is illegal and is penalized by the loss of down and of five yards.   (pp. 33-34)

37   The score is kept by the lineman; pregame procedures and the 25 second count are duties of the head referee; and the time is kept by the umpire.
(pp. 35-37)

42   Player A should be the middle linebacker; player B should be a cornerback or safety; C should be the punter or placekicker; and D should be a rusher.
(p. 41)

51   For the A situation, anticipate a conservative running game. For B, anticipate a try for touchdown or much yardage. For C, expect short passes or short runs to make the yardage needed for the down.   (pp. 47-48)

74   No answer in text. See Chapter 7 for games involving skills practice.
(pp. 76-81)

85   Among the numerous elements of flickerball that are derived from other sports are: advancing ball by passing and free ball rule from basketball; the type of ball, scoring methods and downs from football; some terminology, use of punt, place kick, and passing from speedball; use of penalty box and terminology from hockey.   (pp. 82-90)

89   See these pages for a complete list of dead ball situations.   (p. 88)

QUESTION ANSWER KEY

True-False

1. F	7. F	13. F	19. F	25. T
2. F	8. F	14. T	20. T	26. T
3. T	9. F	15. T	21. F	27. F
4. F	10. T	16. F	22. F	28. T
5. F	11. T	17. F	23. T	29. F
6. T	12. T	18. T	24. F	30. F

Multiple Choice

1. b	6. b	11. b	16. c	21. a
2. d	7. b	12. b	17. c	22. b
3. c	8. d	13. b	18. d	23. b
4. a	9. b	14. c	19. a	24. a
5. b	10. b	15. b	20. d	25. b

Matching

1. J	3. N	5. O	7. F	9. C
2. E	4. K	6. H	8. L	10. B

index